Ideas & Experiments in Lifestyle Design

RAMI EL-ASHI

ISBN-10: 1481957236
ISBN-13: 978-1481957236

www.ramiel-ashi.co.nr

DEDICATION

For my parents, the king & queen that raised me to go with whatever flow I desired. No limitations. Just the freedom to make as many mistakes as needed in order to learn a lesson the right way. I love you both. I respect you both and owe you everything.

CONTENTS

ACKNOWLEDGMENTS

First, let me begin by thanking my Twitter followers, whose kind words and very many RTs have motivated me to write this book. Your compliments always put a smile on my face and allow me to keep bringing you fresh and interesting content. If I could name each and every one of you by name, I would, but that would take a year. So, I can only offer you're my sincerest apologies. Please reach out to me and I'll make amends.

To those certain individuals that have already shown interest in my book, before me even mentioning what it's about. Your blind trust in me is so highly appreciated. Thank you.

Last but not least, I can't help but mention my parents once again, Samih and Amna El-Ashi, who have guided me, encouraged me, loved me, consoled me through my ups and downs. I love you more than words can express. It's that blind faith that means the most to me. Not once have you said no to me, except when teaching me right from wrong. And for that, I thank you from the bottom of my heart.

1 INTRODUCTION

Welcome to my tangible blog. You may be wondering why on earth someone would make a book out of his blog? Well, let me briefly explain my reasoning. I've been known to be a rollercoaster with my blogs. I could set one up one week and the next week I could decide to completely delete everything, not leaving a trace. However, this current blog (www.ramiel-ashi.co.nr) has lasted longer than expected and my readership has expanded to the 80K+ range. Which I assume is pretty good, no? In any case, the main reason behind this book is to preserve the posts I truly enjoyed writing and sharing with you via the blog and to have it all in one convenient book.

I hope it works the same way for you. If you ever need some motivation or ideas on how to make money or make a drastic change to your lifestyle, then I hope this book has designated shelf space in your library.

Please note, that this is not a copy and paste of my blog of course, there are sections in this book that will never appear on my blog (e.g. the chapter on 35 ways to make money and much much more). I want these ideas to be exclusive to the readers of this book. Some of the posts on my blog have actually been re-written for this book, so you'll find extra details you won't find on my blog. So, please do not look at this book as a rip-off, because there is a lot of fresh content here that will definitely help you with your business. I can also guarantee that by the end of this book, you will ALL have your own business. That is of course if you choose to follow the points I have clearly laid out for you. I have given you enough information to no longer have excuses. I have shared secrets I have never shared with anyone. I've let loose because I believe in earning Karma points by helping others.

Initially, I wanted to write a book book, you know, the once upon a time type book, then I realized I was kidding myself. I have no clue how to keep a story going unless I experienced it myself. There will in fact be a story in chapter 3 of this "book" - The Twitter Scam. Which is quite a popular post on my blog. I've been asked a million times, "did this really happen?" I can assure you it did.

I really want this to be a reference book of evergreen content that you can refer to at any time. Most of what is mentioned in this book, I have tried and tested (except for starting a country, but I'm in the process). Just as much as I hate people wasting my time, I do not intend on wasting yours. I will at times throughout my chapters make some absurd assumptions, and I'm just going to ask you to forgive me from the get go.

Take each chapter of this book as you would a blog title. There is no flow between chapter 1 and chapter 2 etc...however the book and blog as a whole have a central theme along the lines of lifestyle testing and improvement. I will discuss travel, education, money, and much much more. I truly hope you enjoy the tests and journeys and I assume some of you will actually try to do some of them, in which case I hope you share your journey with me on the blog.

There will be a new "Books" tab added to my blog which will include all of the resources and downloads mentioned in this book. Feel free to use the comment section of any of those posts as your point of contact with me. You can find me on Twitter too (@ramielashy).

Please enjoy!

2 START YOUR OWN COUNTRY

Let us begin with one of my favorites. I truly enjoyed the process of writing this post (as crazy as it is). The idea that it is possible to start your own country is mind-blowing to me, so I thought I'd at least give it a shot. So, let's begin.

Step 1: Know the rules

In order to form a micro nation and create our own rules, we must follow established rules and conventions. Much of the basis for current nation building comes from the 1933 Convention on Rights and Duties of States, also known as the Montevideo Convention. These are the basic rules set out in Article 1 of the Convention:

The state as a person of international law should possess the following qualifications:

- A permanent population
- A defined territory
- Government
- The capacity to enter into relations with the other states
- The balance of the first ten Articles go on to explain that the existence of a state is independent of recognition by other states, and is free to act on its own behalf—and that no state is free to

intervene in the affairs of another.

- Note that these are not laws in the conventional sense. We are free to declare ourselves a country, anytime, and anywhere. However, nobody will take us seriously, which translates to the simple truth that we will have no legitimacy as a nation (this can change…keep reading).

Step 2: We need to find a territory for our micro nation

I won't lie to you, this is going to be the hard part. Just take into account the fact all existing land has been claimed by existing countries. Wait. Except for Antarctica. Even then, should you brave the weather and lack of "population appeal," Antarctica is managed by the most powerful countries in the world, and it's unlikely they'll let you just plant a flag and say, "Mine!" Still, there are things to try, to get around this dearth of available dirt:

- Conquer an existing country. There are many small island nations dotting the Pacific, and it's unlikely they have much of a defense force. Sure, it's crazy—but crazy enough that it might just work! All we need is an army, a navy, and the support of the world community—many of whom protect these small nations from intruders. This has been attempted in the Cormoros, Vanuatu, and the Maldives, but ultimately failed.
- Buy an existing country. If we are serious about this, we can club our money together and buy a private island (it's cheaper than you think) in fact I once proposed this to a group of wealthy investors as an investment option in one of my projects (but I won't discuss this here), though it's unlikely that the host nation will just cede sovereignty to us. A more corrupt or destitute country might be more easily swayed, but even that is difficult: a pack of libertarians tried to buy Tortuga from impoverished Haiti, but were rejected. There are some things money just can't buy.
- Find a loophole. The Republic of Indian Stream, for example, was founded on land between the U.S. and Canada that was poorly defined in the 1783 Treaty of Paris. It lasted from 1832 to 1835, when it was annexed by the U.S. I don't know about you, but I really can't be bothered to go through years of treaties to find a maybe loophole where we end up getting annexed. No thanks.
- At this point, you might be thinking there's no hope, but I've saved the best for last. As land has become scarce, but the human need for new land continues apace, creative (and financially abundant) individuals have begun taking to the sea. Keep reading!

Step 3: Build an Island!

The ocean, as they say, is the last great frontier. International waters are owned by no nation, and this has spurred interest and activity. Here are some micro nations that have done just that:

The Principality of Sealand. Sealand, initially created as a military base in the North Sea, off the coast of England during World War II, is a football-field-sized structure that housed troops and weapons to strike at German invaders. After the war it was abandoned until 1966, when a rogue DJ named Roy Bates—tired of battling the British government over his pirate radio station—moved there to set up shop. The station never went back on the air, but he declared the floating fortress the Principality of Sealand. He raised the flag, named himself Prince, and his wife Princess Joan. Sealand withstood court challenges, and remains an independent nation to this day. Although not recognized by the "international community", Sealand intrigued me. I mean all in all I think it's tacky trash in the middle of the ocean, but the concept blew my mind. I would make it look so nice. So I decided to do a little more research on Sealand and I smelled a scam somewhere…Yes, it is in its own right a mini-country but they do not have the right to dish our Royal Titles left, right and center. I mean they are offering the public to become Counts, Barons, Baronesses, I mean sure it sounds cool, but according to true aristocracy, you cannot actually sell titles. It has to be your right by blood linage. They are making crazy money out of this because the story of Sealand is so awesome.

The Republic of Minerva. One millionaire activist piled sand onto a reef located in the Pacific Ocean south of Fiji and created an artificial island to start the Republic of Minerva. But since we're not rich enough to make land, then we can just make it up—some of the more lighthearted micro nations claim land on imaginary continents or planets. Anything goes when it comes to micro nation creation.

In addition to the traditional territory-based nation, there exists a largely untapped, unregulated, and unexplored territory that is virtually limitless—because it exists only virtually. Call it the cloud, call it the web, or borrow from William Gibson and call it cyberspace, people are spending more and more time connected emotionally and interactively with their friends and colleagues through the internet. Virtual worlds such as Second Life and Blue Mars create 3-dimensional habitats, have their own currency, and their own constitutions (aka "Terms and Conditions").

Now we're talkin'! Some of these options are seriously viable. We can create an online nation if we fail at building our own real Island, so that's that.

Step 4: Invite our friends

One of the key requirements for a nation—aside from territories—will be a population. If the land we conquer or build doesn't come with an indigenous people, we will have to bring our own to the party. So, let's invite our friends and family to join us in this venture, and we will have a small, but dedicated population.

- These days, if you're serious about anything (and creating a micro nation can be serious, indeed), then we will have a website. We will use this to find like-minded people, and give them good reason to populate our new Republic. It could be for work and money, or the freedom to have many wives, or simply the opportunity to be part of the birth of a nation.
- We will need to decide what we require of our citizens. Do they have to pass a citizenship test, or abide by certain laws? What form of identification will they need—a passport? Driver's license? Subcutaneous RFID?

So, I'm going to take this opportunity to get the ball rolling from the get go and invite you all to join my experiment in creating an awesome micro nation. Whether it happens or not, this could potentially turn into a viral discussion topic across the globe in which we can still benefit in MANY ways. If you are interested in being a part of history, then sign up on my blog.

Step 5: Establish a government and a constitution

The success or failure of our venture will be determined, in large, by our leadership in governance. Consider the success of the United States, rooted in a Constitution that is at once clear and defined, yet open to interpretation and growth. Without that, it may have fallen into disarray and dozens of small nation-states rather than an arguably united whole. Our government, and our constitution, should be guided by the principles we wish to establish from the start. Here are some examples of various micro nations, and their founding principles:

- **Nova Roma**, dedicated "to the restoration of classical Roman religion, culture and virtues".

- **The Aerican Empire**, based on a strong sense of humor and a love of science fiction, fantasy, and games.
- **Political simulations** or political movements. These micro nations tend to have strong political views and are often controversial. In the past, some of them have managed to attract media or political interest, although this is rare. Despite their relative obscurity, they are some of the most common types of micro nations.
- **Cultural missions**. These micro nations, similar to historic projects, exist to promote a particular culture and tradition. There are many Germanic micro nations such as Domanglia that attempt to recreate the culture and traditions of the former German Empire. Many of these also include nationalistic and patriotic projects.
- **Secessionist entities**. By far the most serious form of micro nation, secessionist entities are often much older than other forms of micro nations. Notable secessionist micro nations include Sealand, the Hutt River Province, and Freetown Christinia.

Can you see how much fun we're going to have? The possibilities are endless, but I'm definitely not going to do it myself. We have to work on this together!

Step 6: Declare our independence

Since its founding in 1945, membership in the United Nations has become the gold standard of international legitimacy. When you are admitted to the U.N, that's a form of approval, Talmon says. It's like a stamp [that says] you are now a full member of the international community.

Applying for U.N. membership is a breeze. According to U.N. rules, all you need to do is write a letter to the secretary-general requesting membership. These letters are remarkably short and simple. For a handy template, check out the successful application of Montenegro.

We can then simply mail our application to:

Ban Ki-moon
Secretary-General
The United Nations
First Ave. at 46th St.
New York, NY 10017

Now comes the hard part. The Security Council must refer us to the General Assembly, which must determine by a two-thirds majority that we are a peace-loving state that can carry out the duties of the U.N. Charter.

It's probably not even worth trying this unless we've already made a massive name for ourselves via social media. A number of unrecognized states have applied for U.N. recognition over the years, including American-Indian tribes, but without the credibility bestowed by bilateral recognition, these applications are usually just filed away.

The biggest obstacle to U.N. membership is power politics. Neither North nor South Korea got U.N. membership until 1991 because of vetoes by one bloc or another during the Cold War. Even today, Russia's veto on the Security Council will probably prevent Kosovo from gaining a seat at the table anytime soon. The Republic of China, a.k.a. Taiwan, was one of the founding members of the United Nations and once had a permanent seat on the Security Council. But Taiwan was booted out in favor of the Peoples Republic of China in 1971, after U.S. President Richard Nixon decided to cozy up to Beijing. The Taiwanese government has applied for membership every year since 1993, but to no avail. The United Nations didn't even bother to open Taiwan's most recent letter.

As you can see, the point at which a territory officially becomes a country is very much in the eyes of the beholder. International recognition can be an elusive prize. The good news? The longer we wait, the better our chances become. In international law, which is often based on custom, the longer you can maintain your de facto sovereignty, the more likely you are to be accepted. (Unless, of course, you're Taiwan.)

The strength of Kosovo's bid for independence from Serbia is based largely on the fact that it has, for all intents and purposes, been independent for almost a decade. In a more extreme example, the 900-year-old Sovereign Order of Malta has diplomatic relations with 100 countries and observer status at the United Nations even though its entire territory is contained in a few buildings in Rome. So we shouldn't be discouraged. Starting our own country isn't impossible. It's just going to require a lot of patience and the right friends (which I have).

Step 7: Establish an economy

If we're not trading in dollars, Euros, or other currency, we will need to create our own financial system. Sealand has actually pegged their currency to the US doller, which I thought was odd. While our word may count among our friends, for national debt, we will need some serious collateral for that to be of any use. If we stick to established currencies, we will still need to determine how to fund our government, and the best way to do this may be anathema to the very reason we start your own country: taxes. Through taxation, our government will be able to provide essential services such as a power grid, water lines, a necessary bureaucracy (as minimal as we like), and an army. It's a fundamental obligation for every state (small or large) to be able to defend its citizens from enemies. Whether this is a standing army, national guard, compulsory service, or some other defensive solution, this will be something to consider when creating our constitution. Of course if we choose to do this online, maybe we'll set up a password or something.

Step 8: Be recognized by the world community

Barring any untoward issues resulting from the founding of our country (see above), we will want to become a player in the world. To do this, we will need other nations to recognize us. This will require us to become adept at international law, politics, and diplomacy. If these are not among our strongest skills, we would be wise to recruit a cabinet of skilled politicos to take on this task. This is perhaps the most difficult step of all. Some nations, such as Palestine, Taiwan, and Northern Cyprus have all the checkboxes checked—but are still not recognized by many countries. There are no rules here—every country has their own standards by which they determine recognition. Things that could have an effect on the outcome are issues such as where we stand on al Queda, or communism, or capitalism. They might hinge on our approach to human rights, or control of natural resources. In the United States, the decision to recognize a nation is made by the President. Our request will hinge on who occupies the White House at that time, and their policies and preferences may swing wildly every four years. Don't know what Obama will have to say about us, but he'll definitely hear about us.

Step 9: Manage our branding

Every country needs a flag, of course, and ours will be no different. This is the most prominent of national symbols, but there are other symbols that will help establish our identity as a nation:

- **Money**. What will our currency look like? Will it have my profile boldly embossed on gold coins, and in 3D hologram on paper money, or will we use a symbolic icon such as Lady Liberty or

Charlton Heston? Will we go full-tilt modern, or attempt to hearken back to a time when each piece was carved by hand?

- **State Seal**. We can create a faux-Latin phrase such as E Succubus Opes or some other fancy-sounding phrase, and add some florid graphics with a shield, all to suggest we're descended from royalty (Sealand did this)—or we can state our mission clearly in our own language, and have a graphic designer create a logo. A good logo can be worth more than the crown jewels of England!
- **Official correspondence**. With all the letters we'll be writing to the President, the UN, the Prime Minister, and other heads of state, we'll want a nice letterhead on high quality paper, embossed with our seal.

Step 10: Go out there and do it!

The world isn't getting any bigger, and governments aren't getting any smaller (no matter what they promise), so the sooner we get out there and stake our claim, the sooner we can declare ourselves Prince, King, Emperor, Ayatollah, Supreme Ruler or President for Life of [insert our imperial dynasty here].

I know some people take ideas like this lightly, but the idea from this book is to give you outrageous ideas that have worked, but give them a twist or two to generate exotic sums of money in the process. As I mentioned above, Sealand manage to monetize their "country" but selling you a piece of land. I can't image you getting much land for 19.50 British pounds, maybe a patch of grass? So, we're going to be smarter and apply for a .wc (weird country) TLD. Sell millions and millions of domains to our fans. Keep some for ourselves as sort of back real estate, then as Google if we can have a Googl.wc just to make things that much better.

3 THE TWITTER SCAM: 1 YEAR OF MY LIFE WASTED

Those of you who have been following me for a while on Twitter have followed what seems to be a successful young Palestinian man in his late 20's who lives in Hong Kong and seems to have everything under control, right? WRONG! Well, maybe not completely wrong, but at least in this instance, I failed miserably.

Remember, I'm not a professional writer, and so you need to take what I'm about to share with you with a light heart. There may be some swearing involved, simply because I am remembering this epic waste of time. With that said, I'm just going to wing this post with the hopes that you will get the general picture of what I am trying to convey to you.

Ok, let's start with a quick back story: Back in 2010, I was working for the world's largest oil company (Saudi Aramco), I was two years into the beginning of my career and boy did I have passion. I was literally running in the office. Excited about life and my future. I was making a decent salary (for a guy who hadn't graduated yet) and was well on my way to becoming the cocky, arrogant individual you see before you today. 2 years before that, my parents had started the typical Middle Eastern process of suggesting that maybe it was the right time to start looking for a wife, and well, I couldn't help but laugh. Wife? Why? I'm still too young to go to jail.

Secretly though, it had always been a thought in the back of mind. I am naturally intrigued by marriage and I have always thought that starting a family from a young age is probably quite beneficial for my future offspring. Was I going to find a wife to marry in Hong Kong? Probably not. Why? Because I know all the Arabs here and there is no one suitable.

I had previously had a 1 year "love fest" on Twitter with a beautiful Moroccan lady, who shall remain anonymous. Don't ask. It didn't end well. Moving on…Keep in mind that this post is actually about a SCAM (or should I say potential SCAM) that happened to me, so let me get on with it. I was sitting in the office one afternoon. All my work was complete, so I signed on to Twitter. No I lie. I'm always signed on to Twitter. I suddenly receive a message from a girl with "Flower" picture o.O

Now, if you haven't already seen me mention this a million times. I HATE people with egg profile pictures and I equally dislike those with flowers or anything similar. If you don't want to be seen on Twitter. Then just lurk. Don't tweet. Just troll in the background. OR simply stay away from me and I won't bother you. Ok, back to the message. It was simple: "Hi how are you?". I thought to myself, "ok Rami, stay away from the flowers & eggs, no. Bad boy, don't be tempted, don't answer". I never responded with "I'm fine". We exchanged a few polite pleasantries and I went straight with, "please send me your photo so I know who I'm talking to". *Please note, this was the stupidest thing I have ever done in my life.* She sent me a picture of a beautiful Afghan girl who lives in New Jersey. Of course she did!

Back back story: My parents would NEVER let me marry an Afghan girl. EVER.

Ok, back to the main story. We immediately started chatting and so came a point in our Twitterationship where we decided to hop on Skype and have a "telephone" conversation. Wait, what? No video? HOLY SHIT RAMI! It didn't cross my mind. I was so excited to talk to this girl that video seemed to be unnecessary. We spoke for hours and hours about life, dreams and all that stuff one discusses.

She tells me that her family is linked to Afghani royalty and that explains the exquisite richness she apparently has in her life. So far so good. I'm already thinking, I'm going to get married to ROYALTY! Just a heads up if you don't know me too well, once we get along and I begin to fall for you, I'm already thinking about marriage. So don't give me that "you're freaking me out" shit. If you fall in love with me, you are thinking the exact same thing. It's a logical next step (but not on Twitter - let me tell you).

We talked some more, and I began advising her on a business venture that

14

she had dreamed of and we were set. She wanted to open a small bakery in New Jersey and I was the man for the plan. I made her a pretty nifty blog for her bakery and she registered the company (see the blog here) and we were on track to opening her dream bakery.

A few months went by and I am told she has a sister and two brothers. Ok, I found it a little dodgy that she didn't mention them from the get go, but ok. She also tells me that her parents are flying back to Afghanistan on a charity mission (because they're rich, they can afford to fly off and do things like that). Ok great. What's the relevance of this? Wait wait. I have to tell you something before they return from their trip. Her grandmother had just passed away (of course when I was talking to her) and I was left to heal her heart. OF COURSE! Rami is just too damn nice.

I took just under a month of my life just to calm her down and this is when shit starts to hit the fan. I get a call at work. WOAH! Time difference. America-Hong Kong. This must be serious. I usually NEVER pick up the phone for personal reasons while I'm at work. "Hello, Rami". "Yes, Saliha, what's wrong?" "My parents haven't called for a week and they were supposed to be back!" I do the whole "I'm sure everything is fine. Wait another day then try and call them again, it could be anything".

YOU WON'T BELIEVE what happened two days later. "Rami, there was a huge explosion and both my parents were killed". *tears tears tears* her not me.

Now I begin to wake up. What are the chances on God's green earth that just after your grandmother had died, both your parents die a month later? Of course God has his plans for everyone and I'm a true believer of that, so I decided to continue with this relationship. Take into account that I have now already mentioned this girl to my parents and my intention to marry her. HOLY SHIT!

My parents are now concerned, they are asking me about her and I tell them the story, well at least the part where both her parents die. My Dad felt sorry for her and mother being the bright Palestinian woman that she is, basically looked at me through the webcam and told me I was stupid. Thanks ya mama.

I spent the next couple of months of my life comforting this girl until she had started to feel better. She told me that as her father was a well known heart surgeon in New Jersey, they were holding a huge ceremony to mark his death. Guess where?! Wait for it. Wait for it. HONG KONG!

Ok this is just ridiculous now. You and your sister are both coming to Hong Kong to attend this event? OF COURSE THEY ARE! Wait wait, you're probably dying to ask me if I've seen this girl yet. NO I HAVEN'T! Not once in this whole story did I ask her to just switch on her damn web cam. We just talked talked talked.

Anyhow, her brothers had booked a hotel room for the two sisters and it was time for them to come. I said forget web cams. I can just see this girl face to face when she arrives. Ok. So far so good. The day comes and I have a serious butterfly feeling in my stomach as I make my way to the airport. I arrive and wait.

And wait. And wait. For eight hours! NOTHING.

I call it a day and head home. I don't have a number for her brother's and the two sisters are not responding to any of my emails. Shit. The only thought that went through my head was: "I'm scared for MY life". Not their life. MY life. Something clicked in my mind the next morning that this was a MASSIVE scam. 1 year of sweet talk and now something bad was going to happen to me.

I woke up that next morning to an URGENT email from her brother "Amin" (Amin means trustworthy in Arabic and by the end of this story you will understand just why this name is not fitting) stating that the two sisters were stopped in Canada because her sister's name matched the name of a murderer in Canada who had just killed a girl in some suburb. WHAT NOW? Excuse moi? And now they would have to wait a day before they cleared her name. At this point I had given up on the whole thing and just let it go. No no. There is more.

The day after, I wake up to ANOTHER email from the brother saying, "I'm sorry Rami, I know this is going to be hard to believe, but my sisters have been abducted and have been taken by family members that want our father's money". Hahahahahahaha eat shit buddy. I'm outta here! And I never contacted the brothers again.

A month later, my mother had found me a beautiful young lady and I was ready to put this madness behind me. I flew to Cairo, Egypt. Met the girl and was on my way to getting engaged when I received one final email from Saliha's sister while I was driving the car to my fiancé's home.

You are NOT going to believe this.

"Dear Rami, thank you so much for taking the time out of your busy life to take care of my sister. We both made it back to New Jersey safely after the horror we have been through. My sister (Saliha) was immediately admitted to the hospital because she was so weak and unfortunately she didn't make it".

THE END...

The end my ass. I was speechless. I was reading this email literally 20 minutes before I was to be engaged! I didn't really know how to react, and my life was about to change. I blocked it from my mind (using my amazing power of in one ear, right out the other). That evening, I went home with a ring on my finger and jumped on my laptop and began my research (which is the one thing I LOVE doing). If I want to find out something. I WILL.

Step 1: Background checks

There was never a step 2. From my background checks based on the email addresses I had communicated with for 1 YEAR!!! I came to the following conclusions:

All three email address (Saliha, her sister, her brother) all belonged to the same owner. Can you guess who this owner was? Saliha! But with a different last name. She did indeed live in New Jersey. Get this. She was 45 years old.

THE REAL END.

Moral: Seriously be careful of who you talk to on the internet. It's not as safe as you would imagine. There are some sick people in this world and I experienced it firsthand. Honestly, it was one of the BEST experiences in my life. Because of this incident, I am now meticulously careful when I do things. Always do a background check and make sure of the person's authenticity. Even if you can't go into too much detail, at least do a Google search to see what circles they pop up in.

Better yet...just ask them to switch on their bloody cam.

4 HOW TO HAVE A VIRTUAL DATE (PLUS: MY DAILY ROUTINE)

Welcome to another one of my cheeky little posts. This evening I would like to share with you a virtual date I put together for you. Please note, there are many uses for this, but what was initially created as a long distance romantic date, has now developed into a daily routine of mine.

Step 1: Open all three of these links and smile at the pure genius:

- http://www.rainymood.com/
- http://endlessvideo.com/watch?v=HMnrl0tmd3k
- http://endlessvideo.com/watch?v=DIx3aMRDUL4

Ok, great! So now you're impressed and you're face palming yourself because you didn't think of it before.

Step 2: Open up your Skype and call your loved one, you'll want to use the "Share Screen" function and open the Fireplace to full screen so that you are both looking at the fire together. Smoochie smoochie.

Step 3: Prepare a fine dinner on both sides and pop a bottle of your favorite non-alcoholic beverage (I'm a Muslim, so you may choose to remove the "non" part). Lower the volume enough so that you can still hear the smooth jazz, but can still hear each other's voices.

Step 4: Enjoy a very romantic long distance evening with your loved one.

Step 5: Say "Thank you Rami" in the comment section of this post on my blog. Similarly, if you found this idea to be completely useless to you, you can share your unhappiness in the comment section of this post on my blog. Please read the "comment rules" before you attempt to be rude about it. Your comment will not see the light of day.

My use for these three links:

I have these 3 links bookmarked on every computer I own. When I wake up in the morning and have breakfast, you will find this playing. It really does wonders! I feel so chilled out before leaving the house.

It doesn't end there though! When I arrive at the office, I open the three links and lower the volume to increase concentration on the work I'm doing and again, it does wonders when you're trying to write something. In fact, I'm listening to it right now as I write this book!

Another thing I like to do is READ while having the music, rain and crackling fire place in the background, it's the perfect feeling combined with a cozy atmosphere.

Last but not least, be creative! This is just how I use it. I'm sure you can come up with all sorts of lovely ways to make use of the resources I have shared above. If you've come up with something completely different, then by all means, please share it with me in the comment section.

5 TWITTER EXPERIMENT: HOW TO GAIN FOLLOWERS WITHOUT FOLLOWING ANYONE

Have you ever wondered how some Twitter users only follow a couple of people but have 100,000+ followers? I spent the last week simply analyzing different profiles, the content they tweet, the wording of their bio and I was surprised with some of the results. This is what sparked this experiment. Before I get into that, I want to discuss some of the reasons the above scenario takes place:

The individual is outright famous (it's really as simple as that). Without trying, they are bound to have a dedicated tribe of followers. Therefore, this point doesn't apply to my experiment. I am NOT famous. I am a lifestyle hacker.

If they're not famous, they are a founder/CEO of a relatively successful start-up and people want to learn from them.
Business/life coaches also do particularly well on Twitter. They guide others, 140 characters at a time.

There is one idea that runs through each of these items: Guidance. People like to follow those who can guide them down the right path to success, love, etc…So with my Twitter experiment, I **MUST** include guidance. Wait, but who do I guide if no one knows who I am, and no one is following me yet?

The Experiment

I will start a fresh, brand new Twitter account and will attempt to gain a mass following. The catch is, I am **not allowed** to do any of the following:

- Follow anyone OR;
- Buy followers (that would just be silly and defeats the purpose of the experiment)

Pretty simple right? Just a normal person, with a new account, trying to gain a following. Ok great! So, what am I going to do differently? After going through various popular accounts (not only famous people), in fact famous people are not going to help me at all with my experiment. The fact that they're famous has already done the job for them. I need to use what's available to me on Twitter, which is:

- A profile picture
- A bio
- A background banner
- A main background
- Hashtags

So a good combination of the above 5 items should in theory get me going. Here's where I'd like to open up the comment section to you guys for your opinions. I would like you to let me know your thoughts on what you believe would be the most effective combination of the above 5 items.

I will post the NEW Twitter account here, once we have decided which direction we're going in. I look forward to hearing your thoughts.

Update:

Ok, so the experiment has begun! I have created a new Twitter account: @Arabianist as promised (no longer available), I will **not** follow ANYONE. I started this account on November 6th, 2012 and so far so good. In a couple of hours, 81 people have followed. Of course if I'd followed people, I'd be hitting a couple hundred by now. I'll keep everyone updated in a couple of days. Is it cheating if I ask you guys to follow? I don't think it is. The point is, this needs to be done in a way where I don't follow anyone (until the experiment is over).

Outcome:

Without using any special sites or following anyone at all, I managed to raise awareness of my @Arabianist Twitter account to 500+ followers using smart #hashtags. Would I ever do this again? NEVER! It was a waste of time. Required way too much effort to get a return of 500+ untargeted followers which I hated so much that I shut the account down immediately. Was the experiment a success? Yes! You can certainly raise numbers on your social media accounts by using tags and that's what I did with that account.

In any case, I'm on a new Twitter & Facebook experiment which you can find in a later chapter and that one was a straight out success because I allowed myself to use special sites to gain followers. The goal however was NOT to follow anyone in the process or buy any followers. At one point the account reached 2,300 followers and has now dropped to 1,8xx. Which is not bad at all. I have stopped doing anything on that account and am no longer using it, but I didn't delete it yet. You can visit it and check out that the majority of the followers are real, not targeted, but if I kept on going, I would have had an authoritative jewelry account.

6 MY FIRST EVER BUSINESS VENTURE (PLUS: NEW SOCIAL MEDIA TRICKS & EXPERIMENTS)

This is a 3 part post. In other words it may be a long one, so before you get started, get off your seat, head to the kitchen and make yourself a lovely cup of coffee or tea. Or hot chocolate before you begin my journey.

The three parts we will be discussing are:

- My very first ever business venture – here I will discuss the mistakes I made, how I turned them around and the details of how you should go about your potential business ideas
- A Social Media trick that you can use to look more popular/authoritative on Facebook
- Finally I will discuss my latest social media experiment and how it differs from my previous Twitter experiment

Part 1: The Business Venture

It's 2010. I'd just left the oil company I was working for and was hired as a Sourcing Manager at Jarden Corporation. This was the first move to entrepreneurship I had ever made. I didn't quite know it yet, but quickly learned that with a management position at a Fortune 500 company, you are truly given quite the responsibility, whether you're making $15M dollar decisions or firing suppliers that simply cannot keep up with you, you suddenly feel power coursing through your veins. It's a wonderful feeling. However, there is another benefit of having a management position and that is FREEDOM. You are not longer being watched like a hawk. You do whatever you want with your time as long as you get the job done.

Great! So I settled down into this company and had fully calculated my time so as to allow for as much time as possible to be allocated to creating my own "side business" is what I called it. I made sure that all "corporate" decisions and assignments were completed first, to ensure my financial security at the firm, then used every breathing minute otherwise doing research. What was a researching? Absolutely nothing. I had no clue in the world what I wanted to do. I didn't even have an idea for a business. Hmm...

So, I was good at getting corporate jobs, but couldn't think of a simple business to start? Wait, how did I get my jobs? Research and classifieds? Never! Well, in the Asian financial hub of the world (Hong Kong), you never get a good job searching online/newspapers for jobs. Those jobs were reserved for the average. We were always taught that there can be no average in Hong Kong. You're either amazing or you pack up and leave. Ok ok, so how do you get jobs in Hong Kong? Or anywhere else for that matter. CONNECTIONS!

You know someone who knows someone who introduces you to the key player in the work you're looking to do. So, I said to myself, why not try this out with my own business? So I logged onto ASMALLWORLD (an invite only social network for the elite – A place where you craziest desires can come true – a place where ordering a ship filled with oil is only a matter of asking a simple question...you get the point). So I went into the "Investing & Sponsorships" section and scrolled through, until I discovered "Visually Brilliant"! Wait what? A company for sale that provides Social Media Marketing services among other things. So far so good!

- Do I like social media? Check!
- Do I use social media? Check! At that point I had just started using Twitter and I'd been using Facebook since it first launched (when it was only available to select schools)
- Will I make money? Check!
- When will I cover my initial investment? 3 months! I can deal with that.

So I got in touch with the owner and turned into a child that had a million questions. I didn't care who I pissed off in the process, but I ALWAYS like to be sure about something before I take part in it, so I grilled the guy (sorry, can't mention his name) until I got all the answers I needed. I mean back then, spending US$3,000 on something I had no clue about seemed wildly absurd, but the concept just seemed so perfect for me at the time. Ok, great! "I wanna buy your company good sir!" And I did. We drew up an official transfer contract with all the promises and regulations and so forth (also something I knew NOTHING about at that point) I went with the flow and did my research before signing anything.

2 days later…I was officially a company owner with a fully featured website and all the hoohaa. Except there was one vital component missing. How the hell do I use this site? Where do I get the clients? Where do I even begin? Luckily I had included a clause in the contract that he would include ALL existing clients as well as indefinite training until I got comfortable with the situation. And so it began. My new company was to sell Twitter followers, Facebook likes, Google+ 1s, Pinterest Pins, Soundcloud downloads/followers, Public Relations, SEO and every type of online marketing you could imagine. It was mindblowing! Exciting! So much cool stuff that I had no idea existed and I was going to learn the tricks of the trade!

My first question was? What do you mean "sell Twitter followers"? How am I supposed to get them? He said one word to me: "India!". Huh? What do you mean India? He told me that I would have anywhere between 70-100 employees working for me on an order by order basis!

I paused for a dramatic minute, with a face that resembled something like (o.O)

All I had to do was get an order for say 1,000 Twitter followers, or 10,000 likes and send the orders to "my team" in India and they would take care of the magic. OMG! This is phenomenal! I was two steps ahead of this guy with my questions, I wanted to know where he found these guys, so that in the future I could expand and find new employees to fulfill new offerings. He gave me some websites that changed my life!

- www.freelancer.com
- www.elance.com
- www.odesk.com

Ok, next: How do I get clients?

This is where my life further changed. He told me to create a LinkedIn profile with a beautiful but professional girls picture (excuse me? I had never heard of such madness in my life! Create a profile with a girl's picture? Why habibi? I'm a guy, what the hell do I need with a fake account?) He told me it was a psychological magic trick of marketing and that is when Ms. Antonia Perrone was created! Some of you may have met her, some of you will probably go search for her, but Antonia Perrone was my first ever and highest ever money earning account. She has thousands and thousands of LinkedIn connections. She has made me close to US$20,000 and for some reason she still exists!

I'm gonna cut the story short, but I will tell you this. After a great deal of experimentation, I can safely conclude that having a beautiful female do your client capture is over 70% more effective than having a guy do it. So when Antonia succeed, I created the beautiful Amani Haddad. A Lebanese princess who wasn't Lebanese at all, that furthered my marketing efforts into the Middle Eastern markets.

LIFE WAS GOOD! I was employed full time. A had a side business which was fully paid off within the first month and I was streaming. But and there is ALWAYS a but. I felt guilty! It's not fair to pretend you're someone else and convince others to give you their money. I mean in the end you are still providing them the same service, but it just didn't sit well in my heart, so I took this whole business as simply a GREAT learning experience, which opened a gazillion virtual doors in my life which I have expanded into 4 other companies since I closed Visually Brilliant. I also gave up selling Social Media Marketing services, simply because I learned they were fake accounts that got deleted shortly after when Twitter figured out they were fake.

To summarize my experience, I can only say that VB as a company was designed for a darker businessman than me. It was designed for quick money, but certainly not long lasting. However, without this experience, I would not be the person I am today. I would not have learned all these new things. All these amazing new opportunities I can now create were simply due to the learning process I went through when I owned VB. Now that I've grown and fully understand the Internet Marketing space, I have decided to leave it all together. It's too risky and to be completely honest, it's WAY too much work for WAY too little return. There are much easier ways to make huge sums of money without doing half as much work.

My suggestions to you:

As you start your entrepreneurial life, everything you are presented with is an opportunity. Every business someone proposes to you could either make you money, or a learning experience. In the end I can tell you that the

US$3,000 I initially spent was repaid many times over, not only financially, but it was like I had created my own MBA program that not even my classes at Stanford could teach me. TAKE THE RISK!

Part 2: The Facebook Magic trick

Have you ever wondered how some people post a status about their dog farting and that one stupidly useless post gets 200 likes on Facebook? I mean who in their right mind would actually click "like" on a post so absolutely silly?

Enter Likelo...

Likelo.com is a community of individuals like you and me, just regular people that login to likelo.com using their facebook account and instantly we become one big family that likes EVERYTHING about one another. So, I can login and select any of my photos, or any of my feed statuses and allow 200 random people to like the item I select. Once you click "Allow", it takes about 3 seconds before you magically see 2xx likes on that item. It is absolutely useless to me in terms of making money, but in some cases if I am promoting a new Facebook business page or I have something serious to say, I'll switch likelo on to get my existing friends to take notice. Other than that, it is basically a popularity thing, it won't get you anything other than that.

Notice I said "switch" likelo on? You need to be aware that once you allow likelo to access you facebook account, it means that you too will be liking other random peoples stuff, so in order to stop that from happening, I usually go into my facebook settings and disallow likelo from my app list so it can no longer use my account, but it doesn't erase the likes that I just got! Try it out! Have fun with it, and let me know if you have any problems!

Part 3: My latest twitter experiment

Before you get started on reading my twitter experiment, please take a few minutes to watch the tutorial I put together on how I use Twitter effectively and a cool Google trick for those that didn't already know (click here to watch the tutorial).

I am in the process of testing out a new Jewelry & Watch company which is called (Elashy & Co.). It plays off of Tiffany & Co. in the sense that I am looking at similar style except I want to make so affordable that everyone can afford to buy a good looking piece of jewelry and have it delivered directly to their door. Notice I said "testing". Testing is officially my new favorite word. I love testing stuff. I love experimenting. I have also pre-programmed myself to stop getting disappointed every time an idea doesn't work out. So as part of that process, I am testing out two social media experiments:

The first is Facebook and this one is definitely succeeding. If you visit: http://www.facebook.com/elashyandco you will notice that within a very short test period I have raised the number of likes to the 900+ range. I did this using a site called "likesasap.com". Very simply concept. You can do various activities to earn point and then use those point on your facebook page or various other accounts to gain likes/followers/views etc...it's a very typical social exchange website.

My second experiment was the Elashy & Co. Twitter account (@ElashyAndCo). This is not happening as fast as I expected. I needed a way to continue getting followers without actually following anyone else. Initially when I held my first twitter experiment a few months back, I managed to reach 500 followers solely based on the smart use of #hastags. This is one method you can go about raising followers, but since I am focusing on a very specific niche, in this case Jewelry & Watches, I don't have so many #hashtags to play around with, so that didn't work. So, I am now in the process of testing some sites. The first is Socialclerks.com which has raised my account to 200+ and then I used a new site called traffup.net which raised another 200+ followers. While this is still better than nothing, these followers are not the followers I need. These are just random people following me because I earned points on some websites. The idea is to build at least 2,000 of these followers before I begin the next phase of my experiment which is micro following. If you take a look at my (@ramielashy) account, most of you followed me back, right? Take that as a hint! Ok, maybe you actually like my tweets, but there is a psychological phenomenon with the online world which states that you are more like to follow someone with tons of followers than a person who has 14 followers. Don't argue. You are already a victim of this if you're reading this post, because you have to be following me in order to know that this post exists!

Why is this the case? Simple. The more followers one has, the more he/she is associated with an authoritative status. You can't imagine the number of time I've been asked "are you famous?" My answer is always "no". If you don't know me, then I'm not famous. You may think I'm famous because I figured out that smart tactics always get me where I want to go without doing much work. Life is really not that complicated, except for when it comes to Jumana. I cannot yet find a way to marry her, but I will!

7 PATTERN DECONSTRUCTION & WORLD CREATION

We are all (maybe not all) creatures of habit. The majority have some sort of pattern or routine that they follow on a daily basis. I.e. wake up at 7:15am, coffee + breakfast, brush teeth, get dressed, head to work, etc…In my experience of routine, I have made a quick forecast solely based on my personal feelings that it is only a matter of time before I get fed up of this routine and start creating a new more exciting routine to give my life a little umph. If you feel the same way, then this post may interest you and we can all make a change for the "more interesting".

Let me begin by sharing an example of pattern deconstruction and what I mean when I use that term. There's this show in Las Vegas called "The Act". It begins with an extremely beautiful lady on a trapeze. Every man in the audience is pinching himself standing next to his wife. They are infatuated by her smile and skilful acrobatics. She has a gorgeous face and a great chest. She is wearing a long flowing dress and the room is in silence watching her. The women are jealous and the men are standing like statues. As her part comes to an end, she pulls off her skirt and…

She has no legs.

Hands are brought to mouths. The sounds of "gasps" cross the room and some even scream. Every act of this show is like that. In fact, calling it a show would not be fair. It's an experience. It's an experience that destroys the very pattern you came in with. You were expecting a typical Las Vegas show, and in the end, you got an experience that would probably last quite a while. You may even return home and tell your family and friends about it and so the word spreads like a plague (viral). So now, why wouldn't you want to create a similar concept for your business? Why wouldn't you want your life to be several sets of experiences, rather than just shows? I mean hey, if I could go away from everything I do with that "wow" factor, how great would my life be? I would have endless content to socialize with. I would be a highly experienced individual and I would probably be extremely happy with my life (which is my ultimate goal – 1) being happy 2) making those I care about equally as happy).

Great! So now you've got a basic concept of pattern deconstruction, let's move onto "world creation". The first part above is simply the audience side of this theory. There is obviously the creator's side (you and your business). This requires creativity and hard work, but keep in mind, if you succeed in creating an experience for your clients, you are kindly rewarded by extremely viral advertising of your establishment and in turn you become a happy chappy or chappiette.

So how are we going to create an insane experience for our clients? How are we going to make them say "wow" when they're done? Ok, let's create a scenario for a restaurant. I want you to imagine you're a restaurant owner. Ok? How are you going to create a world where you completely eradicate your client's pattern for one evening? Maybe I'm taking it a little too far with the eradication and destruction, perhaps we stick with deconstruction. How are we going to deconstruct our client's patterns for one evening? How about we start by creating a pop-up restaurant? For those of you that don't know what that is, it's the idea that the restaurant is open for one night only (sort of a surprise) and the next day it doesn't even exist. Note that this can happen with shops too. You just need to make sure you plan this so that everything is mobile and you can move onto the next city when you wish.

Nice, so we've got this pop-up restaurant, is that enough for a wow factor response? Umm…no. I wouldn't be swayed by a pop-up restaurant if all it did was offer me great food. I mean it's just another show! Nothing new. I walk in. I eat good food. I thank them. I leave. Done. This is not what we're looking for. We need to make this exciting. We need to go back to the core of our experiment which is pattern deconstruction. Ok, picture this. It's Friday night. People are dressed to impress. They're ready to kick-off the weekend and you are about to give them a crazy experience. They hear that your restaurant is coming into town (via good PR & Marketing) and a line begins to form at your chosen location. Everyone brings their partner for a great dinner. Husbands & Wives, Boyfriends & Girlfriends, the line is long (if this happens, you could take it one step further in the future and make these pop-up events exclusive. An invite only affair. That is not necessary at the moment. You are just starting).

As you get to the door, this is where we deconstruct the pattern. You are separated from your partner. Who you will not see for 30 minutes or so after which you will meet again to eat your meal. You are then lead into a dark maze and when you find your way to the end of it, a trap door leads you into a different zone, you are given a mask to wear. The purpose of this mask is depersonalize the client. For once in their lives, they get to experience what is feels like to be completely anonymous. Completely free. Every aspect of this experience from arriving, leaving, going to the bathroom and eating is going to be **opposite to what is expected**.

You could find a desk as your table, which brings the office to the restaurant for pattern deconstruction effect (you are flipping work with dinner). You may even find a key under your plate which opens a desk drawer where you find a surprise that forces you to move to another section with a person you haven't met before because he/she is anonymous. The whole fantasy and discovery aspect is what turns people on. If your idea picks up, you can make an exclusive members only event and you can eliminate rules all together by having your members sign some sort of agreement (depending how far you are willing to go with this). As a Muslim, I would not have the heart to go ahead with an idea like this, the freedoms required here will include alcohol and allowing your partner to mingle with strangers while wearing a mask which can take this to a whole other level, but for those with no scruples, this could really turn into something crazy. A night the people of XYZ town will never forget and the best part is the next day. No sign that this place ever existed.

Was it a dream? I'll let you be creative.

If this is too much for you, then why not start by changing your own life first, to make it more experience based rather than just a show. In fact, let's do it together. Let's start off by listing every aspect of our routines and, for each item on our routine list, let's see what we can do that's **the opposite, or at least different**. The goal is to surprise ourselves. To break our own rules and patterns so we don't get too attached to them. There is one item that I think exists on everyone's list that just needs to be deconstructed and that's "asking". You know that special someone you've had a crush on forever and you just can't find it in you to let them know? It's time to stop that. You are going to tell them tomorrow and just see how that changes your life. Or how about that endless job of yours? You're fed up at work. You are no longer challenged. You feel that your life has hit a dead-end. Well, you know what? Quit! Just stop making yourself miserable. Take a baby retirement (which I will discuss in detail in another post) and just take some time to create new patterns that will ultimately make you a happier person and change your life for the better!

If you are feeling comfortable enough, please share your experiences with me in the comment section below. Tell me what your pattern is today and how you plan on changing it. If you are bold enough to go a step further, tell me how you plan on changing your business so that your client will say "wow" when you're done. If I can help in anyway, just ask me. I always try, but I can never guarantee that I'll give you the answer you're looking for!

Finally, I want you to get excited about life. I want your life to be super interesting, because it's not nice to see so many miserable faces every day. The next time someone asks you "What are you going to do the rest of the day?" I want you to be able to smile at them and say:

"I have no idea. Something new."

8 CHEAP, REWARDING BABY-RETIREMENTS: EXPLORE THE WORLD WITH INTERNATIONAL VOLUNTEERING

The world that we live in from here to Great Britain (Download my first ever Hip Hop mixtape; The P-Funk Mecca Fusion which includes a track called "Back to Tha Basics" on which you will find me rapping like a boss. I produced the music for the whole mixtape and recorded the vocals with a friend in a hotel room [studio] here in Hong Kong) has been known to be a massive playground in my eyes and I plan on playing in it. In this playground you find children acting like adults and the exact opposite. Adults trying their best to be young again. In this post, I hope to give you the tools you will need to take a well needed "baby-retirement".

This post plays off some of the ideas that were discussed in the chapter discussing pattern deconstruction & world creation and you need to be able to do the same with your life when your side of the playground gets tough. I've always been a fan of making new friends on the other side, because the more kids you know in the playground, the better chance you have of dominating it.

What we want to do is find a cheap method to expand our horizons and experience life to its fullest. What is better than traveling? Answer: not much. I love traveling. I equally love exploring and learning new things and why not do that at minimal cost? How you ask? It's really very simple. International Volunteering!

There are two sides to International Volunteering, like almost everything else. The good and the bad. The bad in this case is not necessarily bad for you, but the reason that the volunteering is available is because of some sort of breakdown in society or a natural disaster took place. The good side of International Volunteering is when you volunteer to further expand something of use to the world. I know it all sounds a bit vague at the moment, but I will elaborate shortly.

As a philanthropist myself, I tend to veer towards the bad side of International Volunteering and more specifically war effected zones (i.e. Gaza) which is why I started The Palestine Forever Foundation. Breakdowns of any sort can be great experiences: nervous, communication, etc. They allow us to return to center and to refocus on what it is that truly matters. There are people who dedicate their lives to this and completely retire to tend to the world that so desperately needs us. I wish I was as committed, but in all honesty, I really have quite a bit to lose by dropping everything in my life, so for the sake of this blog and the variety of readership, I want this post to apply to the masses, rather than one group of people that are willing to take a complete plunge into the deep end.

Ok, now that we've got that out of the way, we can move onto our baby-retirements. Now, take into account that I am making a big assumption here, but I will assume that you have enough money to arrive at a volunteering location. This is the minimum you will need to continue reading further. If you cannot yet afford to do that, then you will need to explore money making opportunities before you can enjoy a baby-retirement. For those that can afford the travel costs, then there are many opportunities where your host will cover all expenses for you except for personal spending & partying like a mad person. One such organization is the All Hands Volunteers (visit them here), here's a little bit about them:

All Hands Volunteers is a US-based, 501(c)3 non-profit organization, that provides hands-on assistance to communities around the world, with maximum impact and minimum bureaucracy.

Our Mission: *To provide immediate, effective and sustainable support to communities in need by harnessing the energy and commitment of dedicated volunteers.*

Our Vision: *To be the most effective organization at providing committed volunteers the opportunity to give immediate and sustainable help to communities in need and to those suffering in the wake of natural disasters.*

I will not go into details about the projects, but this is a global initiative and they will provide you with a place to sleep and food so all that's left for you is to spend some money on traveling to the project location and you're set! You are about to jump into the heart of a new culture and you're not going to pay much to travel the world.

In my personal opinion, here are the benefits of International Volunteering:

- Cut Travel Costs
- Be Immersed in a Different Culture
- Meet Fellow World Travelers
- Challenge Your Mind & Body

I mean really, what more do you want from life? The playground is there. You are busy making 101 excuses why you can't leave your home and there are loads of people actively playing some fun games on the other side of the playground! My suggestion…go and play with them. It will only make you a better person.

Here are some other reputable organizations you can play with:

Burners Without Borders

Every summer Burning Man participants (aka Burners) meet in the Black Rock Desert of Nevada to re-engage with our community, and to celebrate shared values of radical self-expression and self-reliance. We celebrate the power of community, honor the importance of art, and enjoy the immediacy of experience. Then we leave – without a trace of our having been there.

But that experience and those values don't get left behind in the desert. They inform who we are, and how we interact with the larger world around us. BWB is a manifestation of what can happen when we take our values off the playa and out into the rest of the world.

Project HOPE

Founded in 1958, Project HOPE (Health Opportunities for People Everywhere) is dedicated to providing lasting solutions to health problems with the mission of helping people to help themselves. Identifiable to many by the SS HOPE, the world's first peacetime hospital ship, Project HOPE now provides medical training and health education, as well as conducts humanitarian assistance programs in more than 35 countries.

Over the past five decades, Project HOPE has demonstrated its ability to develop and permanently institute long-term solutions to pressing health problems, the true essence of helping people help themselves.

Project HOPE remains as committed as ever to addressing the world's new health threats by playing a leadership role forging new alliances among those on the frontlines of health and together seek new solutions.

International Relief Teams

International Relief Teams mobilizes volunteers and distributes medical supplies to support the organization's four missions: 1) domestic and international disaster relief, 2) medical education and training, 3) surgical and clinical outreach, and 4) public health. Since 1988, IRT has provided more than $5.6 million in volunteer services, and more than $112 million in medicines and supplies to families in desperate need in 42 countries worldwide.

Relief International

Relief International is a humanitarian non-profit agency that provides emergency relief, rehabilitation, development assistance, and program services to vulnerable communities worldwide. RI is solely dedicated to reducing human suffering and is non-political and non-sectarian in its mission.

Et Voila! I have given you enough information here to eliminate excuses. Browse through all those websites and select a location in the playground that is our world to take your next baby-retirement. Don't want to go at it alone? Then take your loved ones with you. It will be an experience you will never forget and for an added bonus, check your real & karmic bank accounts when you're done. Your real bank account will not look as depleted as it would after a typical vacation and your karmic bank account will be full of karma. Your heart will feel a lot better and in general you will feel very proud of yourself for helping struggling people across the playground live the lives we all should live.

No I didn't forget. The above options are all disaster relief options (the bad side), and I promised to give you the good side, so here's an experience I will probably go on myself:

How would you like to volunteer at Smithsonian Research Island? It's like heaven on earth.

A visit to Barro Colorado offers the opportunity to discover the splendor of a humid tropical forest.

Barro Colorado, the largest forested island in the Panama Canal waterway, is part of the Barro Colorado Nature Monument (BCNM) and is the site of an internationally recognized biological research station.

The wildlife there is extremely diverse. There are probably thousands of insect species and more than 120 species of mammals, nearly half of which are bats. If you are patient and observant, you will discover amazing things. You will learn about research in progress and about the rich natural history of Barro Colorado. We hope to pique your interest in tropical ecosystems, because you are key to the protection of this natural environment.

Even if it costs me more, I would love to take a trip to a research island. That alone sounds cool, no?

Well, we've come to the end of the post and I hope you got something out of it. If you plan on taking any of the above mentioned baby-retirements, then please let me know which one you chose and why. When you get back, please share your pictures with me. I'm always interested to see what everyone gets up to in the playground. As always, I like to suggest you use the comments section below, but it seems you all prefer to get in touch with me directly, which is also fine, but if you have experiences to share, then why not share them with everyone so they can learn about them too?

9 TWELVE A/B TESTS YOU SHOULD TRY TODAY

If you are looking to squeeze more dollars out of your existing traffic, you need to start running A/B tests. Just really quickly, let me explain what an A/B test actually is if you haven't already figured it out. It's simply A or B tests. You try option 1 and see how it converts, then you try option 2 and see how it converts and you go with the highest converting option. This is habit that will get you far with both your online/offline business. There is no harm in testing, but it should be done in subtle manner.

I have been testing you all since I started my Twitter account. You probably had no idea, that's the point! Although I am not making a dime from you, I am simply doing the testing for other projects and to get my name out there, and so far so good. Fortunately, I cannot keep much to myself, so I have to share some ideas with you. I want to get the idea of "testing" embedded in your brain. Test, test, test everything!

Essentially what I would like to do is get a group of "testers" together on a weekly basis and discuss the A/B tests we setup. Which ones failed? Which ones converted tremendously and which ones are worth another shot with a few changes here and there.

So the 12 A/B tests I am about to share with you are successful ones I have done myself:

Test #12: Make it abundantly clear you're available to help

Although I did not do this test exactly as this example, I just want to make it clear how effective it is to advertise yourself where ever you are. There's this guy sitting at a coffee shop and he's got a massive sticker plastered on the back of his laptop that says "Hi, I build software. Come talk to me!"

He was asked how many approached him because of this sign and he answered "a few dozen within 3 weeks". These types of interactions (face-to-face) is where it's all at. If you look presentable and trustworthy, it automatically cuts your online customer search tremendously. The customer walks up to you, not the opposite. They already know what you're offering, and you can show them on the spot what it is you can help them with. Perfect!

Test #11: Eyes, colors, button magic

I was reading somewhere that Gmail did an awesome A/B test with the colors of their buttons. Although we cannot test as specifically as they do, simply because they have a massive user base, but they were able to test 50 shades of blue on a single one of their buttons to come up with the perfect shade that led to the highest conversion rates. That is amazing to me, but I don't have that kind of readership either, so I would suggest that you minimize your test to 2 colors.

A company called Performable ran a test like this to compare the effect of red and green buttons.

Your first guess is green, right? Nope! Red had the higher click through rate by 21%. This is a very simply test, but you can see how important it is to take every aspect of your business extremely seriously. You would have set it to green and left it like that forever if you didn't do this simple test. Suddenly you're getting 21% more!

Test #10: The free dollar value

You have a business. Or you have a product you want to sell. You know there is a group of people who are interested in what you have to say but they're not willing to pull the trigger just yet. Maybe you're not selling anything and you simply want their email addresses so you can notify them personally when you release a new blog post. The most effective way to attract a new reader to sign up to your mailing list is to offer them something free when they sign up with you. It might be an awesome PDF filled with useful information related to your niche, or a free video tutorial of some sort, it can be anything really.

This is where the test comes in. Should you just mention that you will give them a free PDF or should you mention that you will give them a free PDF (Valued at $300) The words in brackets are what create an increased conversion rate. Although not a huge conversion, 6% is still something. Give it a shot!

Test #9: Get on the time based bonus train

Picture this. You are in the process of writing a book. You don't know how much you're going to sell it for yet, but this test is a two part test. Suppose you initially sell this book for $20.00. The buyer would only get a book for $20.00, ok great! Now how about if I told you that for the first 50 buyers, I'd throw in a few video tutorials on how to make money online? Then for the next 100 buyers, I'd throw in something less valuable, but still a freebie. For those contemplating buying your product, these time based bonuses convert massively (47% according to previous tests). It helps them make up their mind.

Test #8: The trial length sale

Now you are the owner of an online system or software. You know you need to offer free trials, but you ask yourself, "how long should I offer this trial for?" With all A/B tests, there are 2 options. In this case, the first option is a 14-day trial and the other option is a 30-day trial. You automatically believe that the 30-day trial will be more popular, right? Wrong. They both gain the same level of conversions on the front-end. On the back-end however is where you see the difference. Because the trial length is so much shorter, you get a huge surge in usage of your app/software/system because everyone is trying to use it more effectively before times up! If they like it, this should translate to increased sales.

Test #7: The difference between a free trial and a money back guarantee

All these years I've been playing around on the internet, I never cared about the difference between these two terms. I still don't have a definition as to why this works the way it does, but using the term "free trial" will boost conversions up by 116%. The word "free" sits well with the masses. The was "30-day money back guarantee" or "30-day free trial". The latter was the winner by far!

Test #6: Screenshots vs. live demos

You have a new product for sale, whether it's a new software, or a physical product, people/companies have a tendency to show screenshots of their products in action, but then again there is no action involved in a screenshot. A screenshot shows me how sexy your system looks. That's not good enough. I want to play with it first before I decided whether or not I want to buy it. How do you do this? You offer your potential clients a live demo on your site. Give them a demo environment to go nuts on. This has been tried and tested and the conversion rates you'll see are in the 38% range.

Test #5: Do the three-step

We all tend to believe that the less steps one has to go through to get through a task, the better, right? So the A/B test here is an application form on your website/blog. Test A consisted of a 2 page process. On page 1 you would select your plan and create your account, then you submit your payment details on page 2. Sounds pretty standard, but wait...what if we split each action into a separate page? Page 1: select a play, page 2: create your account, page 3: submit payment details. Separating each action nice and clearly onto its own page will lead to a 10% conversion rate.

Test #4: Diminishing Fields

When I first dove into the world of internet marketing, I would create these epic forms on my websites where I'd ask the user to essentially give me their life story in the form of a form. I can safely say this was stupid and no one (including myself) likes to disclose more information than they need to when using the internet. Why? Because they don't know you! They don't know what you'll do with their person information. Solution? Don't ask!
So eventually I managed to reduce my epic form down to 4 fields:

- Name
- Email
- URL
- Revenue

I thought, ok, I've killed this form into 4 fields, no one should complain anymore. This will only take 30 seconds or less to fill out. Thumbs down. Can you spot the error? That's right! The "Revenue" field. Don't ask people how much money they make. They feel judged when you know how much they make. They feel like you may treat them differently based on their status. So I did a quick test and changed the word revenue with an open text box saying "what can I help you with?" – Yes, this skyrocketed conversion to the point that I removed the field all together because I couldn't handle the number of requests sent in, so I finally settled with:

- First Name
- Email address
- Website URL

Note that sometimes people do not wish to disclose their last names either and honestly, what do you need with their last name? Nothing.

Test #3: The scrolling sign-up

This company called TreeHouse noticed that their readers were reading the content and scrolling down and completely ignoring the sign-up button at the top of the page. The first test they did was changing their sign-up button color from grey to green. Granted, that did increase conversions, but not enough. They had to do something more effective. So they had their sign-up button scroll down with the user. You can do this by simply fixing your header so that the sign-up bar is always visible at the top. This tiny change has increased their sign-up conversion by 138%. Do yours today!

Test #2: Videos

If your website requires some usage, or some important concepts need to be explained, then video is the way to go. This doesn't affect me because I'm blessed with a readership that likes to read and a lot of the content I share with you needs to be read and stored in your brain for easy access. There are however many websites that have a visual readership. They don't want to read all your text, so you have to accommodate their needs. You make them an awesome video which explains ALL the content on your site and in return, you are rewarded with a 64% conversion.

Test #1: Add the word "FREE" to your ads

Again, I'm going to us TreeHouse as an example. They buy thousands of dollars worth of advertising per month and they came up with $60 as their Cost Per Acquisition (CPA). That's quite expensive if you ask me. It means that for every person that signs up for my service or buys my product, I have to spend $60 to get them! That's nuts. So they did all the usual testing (colors, verbiage, button locations, etc…) and it still didn't do much to change the CPA. Adding the word "FREE" into the ad however reduced the CPA to $43.

10 THIRTY FIVE WAYS TO MAKE MONEY

This is the "Gold" chapter. A chapter I decided to finally include which doesn't appear on my blog. A chapter which will ultimately eliminate your excuses. I have talked to thousands of people, many confide in me and tell me their deepest and darkest secrets via a short DM on Twitter. There is a running theme that goes through each of these secrets and it's money. Rami I only make $X,XXX per month! Some of the numbers I hear are simply haram ("forbidden" in Arabic) to my ears. Obviously I'm looking at everything from a Hong Kong perspective. $X,XXX will not get you a bathroom spaced apartment in Asia. We $XX,XXX rent here. Our salaries are at least 3 times that just to accomodate our rediculous lifestyles. Sometimes i wonder why I spend this much just to live here. Away from family. Then I realize that the money I'm saving will eventually be spend in the Middle East. So i smile.

Ok, I'm getting off topic. I'm going to use this chapter as an opportunity to teach everyone how to make money. By the end of this chapter, you should have no excuses. If you do. You're lazy and you don't deserve anymore help. I'm being blunt with you, because I'm not going to mention one or two ways. There are literally 10s of 100s of ways to make money on the world wide web. These models have all been tried and tested. Not all by me, but by trusted friends of mine who make a living either by one of these models, or combining a couple of them to create something real nice.

A quick clarification:

This is not a SPAM chapter. I will not be selling you anything. If I do provide links, they will not be affiliate links. You may be wondering why I'm mentioning that. This book will also be available on Kindle, so my links will be clickable.

Some of the ideas mentioned here will have "halo" status. This is called "White Hat" in the Internet Marketing world. Other's will have a shaved head and yellow teeth, also known as "Grey Hat", and finally there will be some ideas here that have devil horns and are known as "Black Hat". These are commonly used terms in the IM world, so please keep them in mind before you continue reading. Regardless what method you're into, they ALL generate a lot of money. When I say a lot, I mean a month's salary in a relatively large corporation can be earned in a day if you do your homework.

That being said, I will only explain briefly what each of these methods are. I am not in the business of spoon feeding you. I'll offer that to my future children. I will give you enough information and terminology here to spark your interest. Once you've found the method you think you're willing to try, then it's up to you to do your reading. Google.com should be your best friend. You can find ALL the answer on that search engine. Deal? Of course I will open up a comments section on my blog to accommodate any further questions you may have about this chapter. I will help you as much as I can, but again, I cannot afford to spoon feed you all the way to success. That's up to you. Please note that these models are in no particular order. I am writing them randomly and at different times. You might find the best ones anywhere down the list.

Are you ready? Let's begin:

1. **Forget my advice and begin your own search.** There are those (like myself) who want to start from square one. They want to do all the research themselves and so they start from scratch. Google.com is home base in this case. Always start there. What are you searching for? Forums. Newsletters. Do a simple search like "Ways to make money online". You will be surprised by the outcome. Everyone and their mother has a way to make money online. Some are worth trying, others...not so much.

2. **Flip #1 around.** This is a trick I have used many times when I first started with Internet Marketing (IM). Take all the research you've done. Shove it neatly into an eBook and sell it. Who do you sell it to? You sell it to the people who are still in step 1! It's really as simple as that. Research is never a waste of time. You already put

the effort in and you know that people are ALWAYS looking for research to be done. Hence the title of "Research Analyst" you find in almost every major company. Forget the company. Be your own research analyst. Build yourself a website and sell your research on making money and you'll be set.

3. **Be absurd.** Have you ever come across the guy that will write your message. Put it in a bottle and send it out to sea? He is now rich. You see, there will always be people willing to pay you money for doing something out of the box. Something interesting. This works on the same premise of buying stars. You feel so special when you buy a star, even though it will to absolutely nothing to improve your life. You just buy it to say that you own a star. How about the guy who advertises your website on his face? He'll charge you $10,000 to write your website on his forehead and each location on his face comes at a different price. All of these people are making money and you are busy making excuses.

4. **Domains.** Ah domains. Just a quick heads-up. This method alone can earn you a living. You wouldn't have to do anything else except expand this method for the rest of your life. Let me begin by explaining what a domain actually is. Simply put, a domain is youwebsite.com or .info or .org, you get the point. It is the location title of your home on the internet. It is not what is inside the home, but the infrastructure. These days however, you can treat domains as virtual real estate. If you cannot afford to buy a building in New York, then why not go ahead and start buying building on the internet. A domain is just that. It's like property. You buy for cheap and sell for a mini fortune. Use sites like:

   - www.flippa.com
   - www.sedo.com
   - www.dnforum.com
   - www.afternic.com

These websites allow you to sell your domain names. Now a quick rule. Single word domains are the hardest to get and are highly in demand. You'd be surprised how much a domain like mushroom.com will go for. You can make anywhere between $10,000 to $100,000 depending on the domain name in one sale. Now if you plan on doing this for a living, you'll have to take it one step further and start creating a portfolio of domain names. It's so cheap to buy a domain name (a few dollars), but there's no point if you buy the wrong name! What you'll want to do is subscribe to important newsletters. Follow important bloggers that many people listen to. One very good place to start is the Harvard Business Review blogs. The people blogging there not only have a large following, but they are making predictions.

True story. I was going to start a business with a friend of mine based on a term mentioned in HBR blog. The writer used the term "Applijects" in his post and so we bought applijects.com because eventually it would be worth a healthy sum of money. Applijects would eventually turn into a project application system where Fortune 500 companies would start forgetting about CVs and offering the applicants projects instead. It's a great idea and has already started catching on. So we bought the domain and threw into a portfolio.

If you're serious about buying domains, then you'll eventually realize that domains are quickly running out. When I mean running out it doesn't mean that you cannot purchase them anymore, but their original price will no longer be available to you because someone has already purchased the valuable names. Have no fear! It's time to become a multi-lingual guru. Why not start buying domain names in a different language? As an Arab, I have an endless set of domain names I can start buying the Arabic language is extremely rich and let me tell you, the new businesses popping up in the Middle East are nothing new. They are replicas of existing businesses in the west, but using an Arabic name. Start buying!

5. **Start a domain buy-sell service.** If you're not into the whole process of managing a portfolio of domain names, then why not go ahead and start a service like the websites I mentioned above? The key here is to offer something slightly different (but better) to distinguish yourself from those sites, otherwise you simply won't find any clients. The idea here is you will charge existing domain owners to list their domain for sale on your website rather than using any of the above. If you are looking for someone to program a website for you, then head over to www.freelancer.com and hire one from India. Extremely cheap and they will make you any website you desire. Simple things like adding extra payment facilities to your site will help distinguish. For example, flippa.com always you to pay via Escrow. This builds confidence in your brand.

6. **Run a domain research service.** These days, one of the first things a new company does is buy a domain. Every successful company has a .com, right? Maybe not all, but let's just say most. Ok, that's pretty easy to do and every business owner is willing to do it. Great! Now what you may not know is, big companies like Coca Cola, etc...will not only buy cocacola.com, but they will want to buy ALL the variations. So for example, cocacola.org, cocacola.info, etc. They will even go ahead and buy all the negative domains related to their brand, for example cocacolasucks.com just to ensure that there is nothing negative being said about their company. This is very common and more and more companies are starting to do the same. So, your service will be to provide them with all related domains for them to buy. If you get big enough, they'll let you buy the domains for them and they can even park the domain with you. Parking a domain is exactly like parking a car. You can leave the domain in a parking lot and you can fill the page with related ads for people to click on if they visit the page by mistake.

Example: many times, people will be looking for something specific, like a dentist, and they might just try typing in dentist.com. If you have dentist.com parked, then they will arrive at a page filled with dentist ads. They will click on these ads and you will make money!

7. **Start your own country.** I had to include this here. I know you've read the chapter about starting your own country, but since it's related to domains, I had to include it here.

8. **Buy an existing business.** Now we're moving away from domains and into businesses. This is a method I use regularly but on the side. I tend not to put my name on the project simply because I'm not really contributing anything. This business model works for people who already have a nice sum of money to invest. I would say that $1,000 should be a minimum for you to proceed with this model. If you visit sites like www.flippa.com you will notice there are hundreds and hundreds of websites available for sale. Some of them may look so tempting to you, but there is still an art to buying existing businesses. Some sales will try to fool you buy using a catchy title. My first rule for buying a business from flippa is to only look for businesses that have existed for 2 years or more. I don't need to buy a company that started last month. That means it's shit and the owner is trying to get rid of it.

My second rule is to look for terms like "Auto-pilot". I LOVE auto-pilot. An Auto-pilot business is one that runs itself. If I got off my chair right now and booked a ticket to hang out in a villa in the Maldives, my auto-pilot business should be making money for me automatically. Look for those. Note however, that auto-pilot businesses will not earn you as much money as those businesses which require you to actually do work.

If you are ready to work hard and expand an existing business, then you will find many great deals. It just gives you a boost to get started. Everything will be in place. Most owners will be willing to give you their existing client list. They will also offer you a training course to teach you everything you need to know about running the business.

Another thing to look out for on flippa is the earnings charts. Learn the difference between revenue and net profit. On the front page, they will share the revenue with you, but what we are interested in is how much money is going to be placed in our pockets at the end of the day. Be careful, do your research. Use the comment section to ask the owners questions and make sure you are using money you can afford to lose when buying ready-made-businesses.

9. **Site-flipping.** Site-flipping is like the international traveler that buys and sells properties on a daily basis. If you're into real estate, you'll know the term property flipping. What it means is, you buy a property, you spruce it up, you give it a quick new coat of paint and you resell it for a profit. You're going to do the same with a flippa business. You're going to buy a business that's making money, you're going to give it a little touch up here and there and you're going to sell it for a profit! Simple as that.

Let's move away from these more automated ideas for a while and take a look at ACTUAL work. The above mentioned methods are still work, don't get me wrong, they just don't require you to do the dirty work, they only require you to manage an existing business (which is my style). However, there are always those who are blessed with certain skills which they can use to also make money. Let's have a look:

10. There are loads of jobs available by the hour. You can find these jobs on freelance websites and will share some of the ones I use

with you, but there are many more:

- www.elance.com
- www.guru.com
- www.rentacoder.com
- www.designoutpost.com
- more

This is probably a good way to get start on making some side cash for lunch, but can be expanded depending on how good you are. If you live in countries that are relatively cheap, then you can make a living out of providing free lance services. However, if you live in extremely expensive countries, then you will make just enough to have a free lunch.

11. **Email or phone answering.** I'm sorry if you think this is a joke, but it's a job. It exists. And you can make money from it. In fact, it can really get quite technical and requires training in some cases. I mean it really depends on the company you work for, but you then become the face of the company. You are the first person people run to when they need help with a product. You can either do it over the phone, and so the client will call you and ask how to do something that's mentioned in the product manual, or it can be an online based chat when the user clicks the "help" button. You are actually saving the engineers a LOT of time and they will pay you for that. There is no harm in taking a job like this if you are not tech savvy. It's still money coming in.

12. **Web design, graphic design, HTML & CSS.** Are you good at any of these skills? Make use of your skills. Start creating templates for existing blogs. For example, create an awesome Tumblr template. Tumblr is exploding these days. Make it so nice that you can sell it for $49. Then sit back and watch the dollar bills grow legs and stroll into your bank account. This is like semi-auto-pilot. It requires you to do the initial work, but once you've perfected that, you just unleash it and watch everyone go nuts trying to get it.

Once you're done with Tumblr, make a wordpress.org template (slightly more professional and requires some more programming) but you can sell these for more. There are so many webmasters and new company owners that don't know where to start with a website, so you need to find them and help them.

13. **Read email.** Sounds boring no? Well, it's a job and it pays. There are companies out there that will pay you to read email. Why? Because they need your eye to catch the SPAM. You're probably thinking, "but I thought there was software for that kinda stuff". The answer is yes there is, but with programs, there is always a chance that false positives occur and depending on the nature of the company, they may not be able to afford to make that mistake, so they'll pay you to make sure everything is funneled correctly.

14. **Faulty batches.** This is a rare but can earn you a fortune. Every once a in a while, actually more often than that, you will find factories that makes slightly faulty batches of items. These items can be anything from clothing to electronics. What is regarded as "faulty" to a factory that is manufacturing for a top company like Ralph Lauren, may look perfect to you. Sometimes these factories have to dump these "faulty goods" and start again. You can negotiate with these factories to take their faulty goods and resell them. Please note we now venturing into "Grey hat" territory. Sometimes you might not be able to resell branded clothing, etc…It really depends where you live. This happens a lot in Egypt for example.

15. **Be ridiculous.** Just be right out nuts and come up with an utterly stupid idea that sounds somewhat cool and hope that it picks up. I know I already mentioned the many writing messages in a bottle and setting it into the ocean, but this one is quite interesting and I have attempted it myself. Go the MillionDollarHomepage and read what this guy did. He created a grid made up of 1,000,000 pixels. He told everyone one he was doing it to collect money for university and proceeded to sell each pixel for $1. He is now a millionaire. Now go check out ClickHereYouIdiot and these $10,000,000 ideas that shouldn't have worked then slap yourself for complaining about not making any money.

16. **Don't be ridiculous and be useful.** Don't feel like being silly and want to be taken seriously? Then find people with problems and help them solve those problems for a small fee. Wait, it only begins there, then people start to remember your name and you are suddenly a sought after business coach! What do you do then? Change those small fees to create a business you can live off of. There are some business coaches/life coaches that earn $1,000/hour because they are so good at helping people out with their lives & businesses. Become a Business Coach!

17. **Become a drop shipper.** This is one of the easiest and most effective business models of all time. Chapter 6 of this book is basically based on this model. Find something people need. Find who sells it for the cheapest in the world. Then offer it to those people for 600% profit. Why? Because they are too lazy to do the research you were able to do. Always try your best to get closest to the source. You don't want this to become a broker chain where you're getting it from a guy who's getting it from another guy etc...You want to be the one and only guy getting the juicy profit from your sales.

18. **Become a blogger.** I bet it sounds ridiculous to you right now. Keep reading. You're probably thinking, "but I'm already a blogger". I'm going to answer now, "no you're not". You're a flogger. You're just reposting pictures of things you think look pretty. "Wow, those shoes look so pretty! OMG, I'm gonna die." Don't be silly. You're not going to die and I'm not amused at all by your blog because I can get nothing from it. I can't buy my future wife those shoes. I don't even know where those shoes were made! All I know is you're willing to kill yourself over a pair of shoes.

No, none of that shit please. I'm talking about becoming a serious blogger. Someone with a healthy mass following in a specific niche. Now this is where your words will make you money. People begin to trust you enough to the point that they will follow your recommendations. If you create something, they will buy it from you. If you're an affiliate, they will buy it from them and you'll make money off it. Your playground expands. Say you don't want to annoy your followers with sales (like me), then open your blog to advertisers. It becomes auto-pilot income. Sell ad space on your blog for a handsome sum of money.

19. **Become a broker.** This is another one of those business models that you can make a living from. If you consider yourself to be extremely social and I don't mean that you have random online friends, I mean you have quality social connections in good places, then you can easily become the middle man. If someone wants something (e.g. a ship filled with oil), but they don't know how to get their hands on it and you do. Then you can broker an agreement between that person and the person you know. Depending on the size of the order, you negotiate a percentage for yourself. Let's call it a "Finder's Fee". This fee usually ranges anywhere from 3% to 15% depending on the deal. You can make

large sums of money very quickly like this. They key here is to be very organized. Stay in touch with key contacts. Make sure they remember you, so the next time you're looking for a ship filled with oil, you can increase your fee. You get my point. This applies to all types of deals you broker.

20. **Surround yourself with opportunities.** Believe it or not, the people you surround yourself with will make your break your ability to make money. I'm not saying you should replace your friends. I'm saying you should start finding those who you look up to. I mean I have my fair share of friends who are on a different planet than me, because every once in a while I need to take a break from thinking about business and just sit back and enjoy a friendly chat with people that care about other things. Granted, at some point I'll take their ideas and probably turn them into a business scenario, but that's just how my brain works.

Then there are those "acquaintances" that I hang out with simply because their minds are pure genius. Most of this group are older than me but with that comes a cave of knowledge and ideas I would have never thought of. Can't find those people? Then the least you can do is find them online and become virtual friends with them. Learn from their writing. Have a Skype conversation with them and exchange ideas. They probably have 101 ideas you never thought of and are willing to let you use those ideas because they have no use for them (at the moment). Take advantage of that can make a move.

21. **Clickbank.** It still shocks me when I find out that some people still don't know what Click Bank is. This is Internet Marketing 101.

What is Click Bank?

I'm going to make this brief. Click Bank is a platform where buyers and sellers meet. The seller has a product or service to sell, whether it's a book about weight loss or pest eradication service, everything goes on Click Bank. You're probably wondering what the catch is. There is always a catch but you can become extremely rich using CB as your weapon.

I will give you an example. There's this guy. He created the most popular product in Click Bank history. A very simple product. A book. The book is about weight loss. I know it sounds typical and very scamy, but this is a weight loss book that actually works. He tested it out on family and friends first and made sure that everyone was satisfied with what the book had to offer. He is a professional instructor and nutritionist. He knew exactly what he was talking about when he wrote the book and called it "Six Pack Abs".

He decided to put this book on Click Bank and let millions of Internet Marketers sell his book for him. Here's the catch. You have to share a certain percentage of your earnings with the marketer that sold your book. Ok, so far so good. At first like you and me, you're thinking something like 10-15% should be sufficient. After all, you put your blood, sweat & tears into this book, so why would you share any more profit with random internet marketers. Well, he had something else in mind. So he began his test. He noticed that every time he increased the percentage, more and more books got sold. And so a 75% percent standard was set. Can you imagine giving 75% of your earnings to someone else who doesn't know you or your book? Obviously there was a lot of mathematics involved in coming up with this 75%, but this gentleman is earning $1,000,000+ a month. That is $12,000,000 a year.

You're now wondering why he was so successful, right? Let me tell you. The other side of Click Bank is the seller side. These sellers choose products they want to promote and in return they get 75% of your profit. How many sellers are there? Millions! You are essentially allowing millions of Internet Marketers take your product and promote it to the world. Some of them are so good at promoting that you'll find your product spread across the world in no time.

I can tell you right now. After this book hits Amazon, I will be selling it on Click Bank too! It only makes sense to practice what I preach!

22. **Webinars.** Know something about something? Create a webinar. Make sure you're an expert in the niche or you will disappoint the people that paid money to watch you. There's this girl called Yaz The Spaz. She runs a Muslim Hijab video log where she teaches girls how to fashionably wear their Hijab. I've even watched a couple of her videos. She has a dedicated following, but does not intend to monetize it. She would be loaded if she just turned it all

into an online webinar for a small fee. This leads me to item number 23.

23. **The Freemium Model.** About a year ago, I was talking to a friend of mine about this idea of freemium and what it actually meant. How does the giver benefit? Does the giver need to benefit? Can freemium actually work as a business model? The answer is a definite yes. However, before we discuss ideas, let us first define "Freemium".

Freemium is the concept that you offer premium services/products for free. For some people this sounds absurd. Why would Rami include it in a money making section of his book? Let me tell you. I was always intrigued by freemium models. I have always given things away for free as a teenager and now that I can afford it, I have started giving away things higher up the premium scale. My last fund raising campaign for example, I gave an iPad away, which I guess is not all that premium these days, but it's a start.

That's beside the point. It's the return from the freemium offer which excites me. I found that the more people I help out for free, the more they were willing to throw money at me. Take that last sentence however which way you'd like, but it's a fact and I'm sharing it with you. I'm not going to sugar coat this. Be nice (for free) and in return, you will get paid because the free services you provided that one time actually worked and they are now coming back for more on a much larger scale.

Take it a step further. Help the right people. Help potential clients. Seek out those people you believe actually need a service that you can provide, then tell them you'll do it for free. When they give you feedback about your service, and that feedback is positive, then tell them you'd be happy to continue providing that service for a "small fee" (small can be as big as you want it to be, it's just a polite term to use when talking to clients).

24. **Fiverr Gigs.** Loads of you will have heard of Fiverr, right? You'd be surprised how many people have no idea that it exists and with those odds, you will make bucket loads of money. This is another one of those methods that I initially started off with.

Just briefly, let me give you a quick background tour of Fiverr. Like the name suggests, Fiverr is called Fiverr because everything being sold on the site is worth US$5. Basically what you'll find there is a bunch of people from across the globe offering you services for US$5. You'll find almost everything you could possibly need, such as: gifts, graphics & design, video & animation, online marketing (yes, this includes Twitter followers, Facebook likes, etc…), writing & translation, advertising, business (this includes business plans, business reviews of your existing business, lots more…), programming & tech, music & audio, fun & bizarre, lifestyle and lots of other "gigs" – the term "gig" here is used to describe an offer.

Ok great, so now we know a cheap place to buy cool gigs. However, what I'm interested in is how am I going to monetize this to my benefit? Simple! We are going to create a cool little Tumblr.com or Wordpress.com blog. We are going to make it look as legitimate as possible. When I say that, what I really mean is, you want it to look as close to a professional website as possible. You want people to trust you immediately. You also don't want to miss all the important information that any professional website has. Make sure you make it as simple as possible for people to get in touch with you. Include an "About" section. A "Contact" section. Make it look like you own a company.

Now for the fun part. Once you have your blog up and running, you can start to populate it with your offers. Take any popular Fiverr gig and re-offer it! Instead of $5, you offer it for $20. Believe me, $20 is the lowest you could possibly make on these offers. I used to sell single gigs for $600 and there are plenty of companies willing to pay you for this type of work.

Where do you find these companies? Linkedin.com is your new best friend. Create a new LinkedIn profile using a profile picture of a beautiful professional girl (read Chapter 6 to learn a little about my experience of using fake LinkedIn profiles). If you're not super creative, you can use a website like www.fakenamegenerator.com to create a full profile history of a random fake name. Each one of these profiles will become "your" employee. Give them titles like VP of Marketing, or Associate, etc…Make them as professional as possible. One issue I came across when doing this was that because my profiles were all female (I did this simply because my experiments have shown me that people tend to trust and respond much more to females than males, especially when it comes to social media) I had a problem when potential clients ask to talk to "me" on the phone. It's a bit odd, but there is a way around this. Simply refer them to someone more experienced to handle the account. Guess who that more experienced person is going to be? Yep, that's right. The REAL you!

Make sure you create an generic email that you will send to each new connection you make and be sure to address them personally. Don't just send a bulk mail to everyone you connect with. Why? Because it comes off as SPAM and that is a very big boo boo on sites such as LinkedIn. They will kick you off immediately. Make sure all your message sound as if you are truly interested to connect with them and that you'd just like to share your work with them, and that's when you include a link to your website.

If they like any of the services on your site, they will get in touch with you. Tell them that you have to accept full payment upfront before you put the order through the system (because you've been burned a few times where people just don't pay). I will promise you one thing and I really hope you'll take my advice on this. Do not ever promise your clients something you cannot provide. I remember when I first started, I used to tell my clients that they'd be getting "targeted" followers on either Facebook or Twitter. That's in all honesty – bullshit. These Fiverr gigs are 100% automated. You want 10,000 Twitter followers? A guy in India will set his computer to generate 10,000 fake Twitter accounts (which include pictures of real people & a bio) but in reality they are blank accounts and tell those 10,000 accounts to automatically follow your client. Of course you're not going to tell your client this, but you're going to make it clear that is not a targeted service and that your packages are strictly for number boosting. This is when you explain the benefits of number boosting.

Number boosting is actually very useful in Social Media, if done correctly. Imagine two Twitter accounts. 1 account has 2 followers on it. The other has 20,000 followers on it. Which one does your mind automatically trust? The one with 20,000 followers on it. Don't argue. It's a psychological thing. The same applies to Facebook pages. The higher the number of likes, the more trust. Also, the higher your numbers, the higher the chances of new followers coming to you, so make sure your client understands all this. It really helps you sell your gigs.

I don't think I can spoon feed you more than this. This idea of reselling something for a much higher profit has always worked for me. Start off with Fiverr at first so you can get a feel for buying and selling and running you own company, then you can move onto bigger items on other websites. Use the LinkedIn groups to target your clients. Be smart when connecting with people. Search for people that are actually looking for a specific service. Check Fiverr to see if that service is available for $5. Sell it to your client for $50. Or $500. Then give your client a "special discount" the next time round. Tell them they're such a valuable client that you're willing to give them a $100 discount. They melt. They tell their friends. And you become the main man/woman to go to for "this or that" service.

25. **Play Video Games.** I never thought I'd suggest this in my life, but since I'm finding way to eliminate your excuses, here's one that you can't argue with. You may hate numbers. You may detest business models. You might not even know what ROI stands for. How about video games? Do you know what they're all about? Yes you do. If you're good at playing video games, you can make at least a couple of hundred dollars a week. Look around your area for tournaments, events and all related game festivals. You can treat this as a side gig, or if your name really gets big in gaming, you can make A LOT of money just playing games. You can also get lots of money off of endorsement deals that come with your name. Do a little research and you can make a career out of it, if you have time to spare.

26. **Mystery Shopping.** This is a concept that is perfect for those secret materialists among us. Wait, who am I kidding. I am definitely a materialist in a sense. I love me some high quality materials, whether it be a nice sweater or the latest in technology, I don't really care what others think of my purchasing habits. I've earned the right to buy what I need when I need it, so just go with the flow. If you're are anti-materialistic, then this particular model is not for you. Mystery shopping is when a company lets you go shopping in their store to analyze their employees. For example, they'll tell you to go out and buy some clothes from one of their stores to see the quality of customer service. Yes, you get to keep the clothes. It's a shopping spree and you get paid in the end. This is not only for clothes shopping, some companies send you on vacations, restaurants, etc…and they pick up the tab as long as you give them constructive feedback about their service at the end of it. Ok, I wouldn't rely on this as career, but in all honesty, if you have

an entrepreneurial mindset, you can always flip something like this to your benefit. Sell the clothes they bought for you. Take a client out to dinner at the restaurant they're paying you to try out. You get my point? Always flip the opportunity to your benefit (if you can).

27. **Become An Agent.** This one is very closely related to becoming a Broker (which I mentioned earlier). This one is more specific. You could become an Estate Agent, but not the real type. You can become a "Buying Agent". Or a "Broker Estate Agent". You don't have to be registered. You don't even have to show people the house. You just need to have more time than the people who are searching for new homes.

    Log into your local property listing sites. There will be several depending on where you live. Look at the items people are looking for. Find a home that you think meets their requirements then keep 1-3% of the property value. If you get good at this, you could easily expand this into your own property search business.

28. **Concierge Personal Shopping.** This requires someone with some energy to run around. Being a personal shopper is quite the job, but you can make money off of it. You target audience will be rich, busy people who would be more than happy to have someone go do their shopping for them. You can do their groceries, you can buy their personal items, you'd be surprised how many things busy people will pay others to do for them. A perfect example of this would be www.domystuff.com. If your parents have a good contact list of people, you can start with them and build from there. When I say build, I mean expand this into a business and start doing the same for companies in your area. It saves them money and makes you more money. Be creative and you can do a lot with personal shopping.

Let's just take a quick break from the normal method of the whitehat wearing people and venture into blackhat territory. I am in no way endorsing the methods I am about to discuss, but I'm merely letting you know that they exist. What you do with them is your business and it will require you to do your own research to find out if you'll go to jail or if you can find a way around it

29. **Find Loopholes.** Let's consider this a little more Greyhat. Find someone who is not following the rules of your blog/website and

sue them. The US has shown us with several examples that you can sue someone for serious stupid things and get paid a handsome sum of money. Be smart about it. Remember companies are more willing to settle a small sum of money than pay to fight it out, so you could use that to your advantage.

30. **Become a Paparazzi.** Obviously living in LA would be a good start. But snapping photos of famous people at their favorite hangout is an option to make some money. Sell these photos to tabloids and be smart about your asking price. If you snap a photo of someone who just recorded their album in their basement, you will probably get the boot. Find yourself with Paris Hilton doing something naughty on video, then be prepared to become extraordinarily rich.

31. **SPAM.** Just SPAM the clickbank products I mentioned earlier to everyone in the world and you're bound to get some sort of response. Is this legal? Not on its own, there are however rules to make SPAMing legal. Like I said, I'm not about to do the research for you, so do it on your own. My final method will be about the smartest SPAMing technique I have ever witnessed in my entire life.

32. **Split test combinations.** This is not so much a model on its own, but it has certainly opened many new doors for me. The first thing you're going to want to do is come up with an amount of money that will make you happy. Let's just go with US$1,000,000 for this example. Right off the top, there are two combinations you can use to get to $1M. The first being, selling one thing for a $1M. That will be impossible for the majority of us, unless we are in the business of selling Oil Vessels (Big Oil Ships). Most likely not going to happen. The other option would be and is very doable, is to sell an item for $1 a million times.

In my experience, this would most likely have to be a digital product (i.e. a book, software, etc…). Selling a physical product 1 million times in your shop could take you a lifetime. If it's done online, things can become replicated. Take for example the method I mentioned earlier about affiliates. They could easily help you achieve these numbers.

These are only two options! Sit down with a sheet of paper and right down every combination you could have to get you to $1M and new ideas will start popping up in your head. This will help you value certain items. It will help decide how you want to market your product. Who can help you. How long it will take, etc…It's a great exercise to expand your horizons.

33. **Go White Label.** You can have your new business up and running today if you want to. Head over to Google.com and search of white label businesses. I realize many of you will already know this term, but for those who don't, White Label means you get a readymade business with a blank label on it (i.e. you get to put your own company name on the header. No one will know that the business is being run by a third party).

This will be my first time to admit this, but one of my first businesses is a white label hosting service called <u>ResellersPanel</u>. In fact it's free! All you have to do is sign up with them and they'll provide you with a site like mine (<u>www.bicubik.com</u>) so obviously I purchased the .com and created my own logo, but all the systems are run by them. They allow you to customize your own pricing and packages for your own clientele. You don't have to buy a .com to own this business, they'll give you a free URL to use, but then again why not make it look as professional as possible?

Your Google search of the term "White Label Businesses" will show you many other options. Want to start your own make-up brand? You can do that with a few clicks. Want to start your own dating site? You can do that with a few clicks, and guess what? It'll already be pre-populated with a huge number of people. I think at one point when I was exploring White Label business, I created my own dating business, but it turns out you actually have to care about the business you start, so I dumped that stuck to my Bicubik.

This is an extremely profitable way to start off your business career.

34. **The $2K/month model.** So far I've given you idea after idea on how you can make money. I wouldn't feel warm in my heart if I didn't spoon feed you once to make 100% sure that I have eliminated your excuses. This model will be detailed and if you follow it step by step, you will be well on your way to making US$2,000/month. The model is also scalable based on your efforts. The more work you put in, the higher the return. There is also an auto-pilot taste to it, which means "look ma! No hands!"

I have personally tried this method, so no excuses please. Let's get started. This model is a combination of online and offline work. Just the way I like it. I like to sit behind a computer, but I also like to get out there and mingle with my clients. It's the best way to beef up your courage and expand your social network. Let me begin by explaining the model in short:

You will be building simple Wordpress websites for offline companies in your area. They are all over the place. Start with your family! My family is very traditional in the business sense. You say www, they say café, coffee and tea. Exactly…not a clue! However, if you ask them, "would you like a website for your business?" They will almost always say yes because they have no choice but to recognize the power of the internet and how it could potentially boost their business a million times over. So, what are you going to offer the newbies? This:

- **Free hosting**
- **Free domain name**
- **Designed website**
- **Facebook business page**
- **Website submission to Google & Yahoo search engines**
- **Easy admin control panel**
- **Built-in search & much much more!**

You're going to offer all that for $49 a month!

What are you thinking right now? Wait, let me guess. "WTF? How?" or "That is WAY too much work for such a tiny sum of money". Well, that's only your first reaction before doing some simple calculations. Let's take a look at how much time and money are going to go into doing all of the above:

- **Free Hosting**. 1 shared hosting package with any company such as GoDaddy.com or my favorite Certified Hosting will be more than enough to host 1,000 small websites. If I'm not mistaken, my website hosting package with Certified Hosting allows me to host unlimited amounts of websites, so you've got the hosting covered.

- **Free Domain**. That'll cost you $10 a year. That's around $0.8 a month. Take note that this will be the only thing you're paying for. If you cannot afford the $0.8 a month, I don't know how you got hold of my book.

- **Custom designed website, Control panel & Built-in search**. That's all just Wordpress doing the work. Install Wordpress on your hosting account has become automated these days. When I first started building my own Wordpress.org sites, you had to go through a horrible process. Today, you simply click on "Install Wordpress" and a minute later you're ready to install your theme. This will all take you no more than 1 hour.

- **Facebook page.** This costs nothing and will take you less than 5 minutes to set it up and include a nice cover photo and logo for their company.

- **Submission to Google & Yahoo**. This is not really anything. Your website SEO will rank you somewhere on Google. It's just a marketing technique to get them on board. Everyone has heard of Google and the idea of them being on Google sounds amazing in their heads.

Total time taken = 1 hour. Total dollars spent = $1 a month! Now remember, in return, you are getting $49/month for doing 1 hour of work + your $1 expense each month! Also, this is a recurring payment which they will probably put on their Visa cards. This is when auto-pilot kicks in. Once you've spent that initial 1 hour building their site, you're basically collecting rent for hosting their website and being in control of their domain. If for some reason they decide to default on the payments, you can stop their website immediately and wait for them to come running back.

Knowing what you know so far, how easy do you think it'll be to find 50 customers? Depending on where you live on this lovely globe of ours, you can easily find more than 50 traditional companies without a website. These are your customers. Fantastical! So, let's just do another quick calculation to ease your heart:

50 x $49/month = ~$2,500/month – sounds yummy, no?

Let's calculate how much time you will need to achieve this. One-time only, you will dedicate 50 hours of your life to make this an automated money machine. That's 1 week of 7 hours per day. That's one hour less than a full-time job and you only have to do this for a month. Once you're done, you can sit back, relax and collect the money. When I did this, I stopped at this point, because

I was investing in other projects. If I was to continue with this model, I would have taken my first payment and hired someone in India to continue the process for me. So the only thing I would have to do is find new clients and the rest would be a onetime payment to a programmer and I'd collect the rest forever.

Now let's get into the nitty gritty. The work that you'll be doing or outsourcing if you take my advice above. The first thing I did, was go through the various free plugins that Wordpress has on offer. These plugins are magical little tools which you can add to the site you're building to allow it to automate things. Don't worry, I'm not going to ask you to start studying the Wordpress plugins page. I've done that for you and have come up with the following list:

- **Add link to Facebook**
- **All in one SEO pack**
- **Contact form 7**
- **Facebook comments for Wordpress**
- **NextGEN Gallery**
- **qTranslate**
- **Quick Chat**
- **Visitor Maps**
- **WP-Polls**
- **WPTouch**

Click on any of the above to read about them in detail. Please note that this is the list I used two years ago. I know these are still valid plugins, but there are many more cools ones available to you, so if you want to expand this business and scale it, you can start offering more and more to your clients. Just keep that in mind when you reach this point in the process.

You're probably thinking now, "how about the theme?" I don't know how to design a theme! I'm not a programmer. I'm not a designer. Again, have no fear, Rami is here. There are millions of websites out there offering free Wordpress themes. They may not be premium themes, but you can find lots of free ones to download. Hint: and you didn't hear this from me, there are also plenty of websites out there that offer premium Wordpress themes for free, you just need to search. Once you've found let's say, 10 different themes, do a quick screen capture of the themes and show them to your clients so they can choose!

Now comes the hardest part. Find your clients and advertising to them. You want to get the perfect amount of information in front of their eyes so it doesn't take them long to understand what you're offering. You can do this by advertising in classifieds, you can actually go door to door and have a quick discussion with them. You can even do an email marketing campaign and just contact them that way. There is also the option of doing a snail mail campaign, if you're not in a rush. A quick trick with snail mail is to add two red dice in your envelope so that it becomes a parcel instead of generic under the door marketing mail. When they open the envelop, they will see the two red dice and will automatically become intrigued. Here's what you'll want to write in your marketing content:

- Hosting & Domain expenses included!
- Free designed Facebook page bonus!
- Control your website easily with your own control panel!
- Built-in search, contact us form, user comments, polls and much more!
- Free professional logo design
- We will submit your website to search engines like Google & Yahoo!
- Free support!

Use green check marks instead of the dashes I've used. Green check marks have been known to convert much better.

Yes, the last part is a must. Remember these customers are not best friends with the internet. They probably won't change anything on the site once you give it to them, but with every service, you must offer your support in order to keep your client satisfied. Make sure you create a brand new email address for your business, so you don't mix it with your personal accounts, and buy yourself a new SIM card for this new business of yours. Tell your clients, that you are currently working with another client and that you'll get back to them shortly. That way, they can see that you're extremely busy and sought after and they'll be happy to wait, unless it's extremely urgent.

Finally, let us discuss other methods you can use to market your service.

- Create a sexy looking flier using the information I gave you above. Print out 100 of them, or however many businesses there are in your area. Give a kid $20 to run around and distribute your fliers to every business. Be sure to include your contact information on the flier (i.e. The new Email & phone number you just created for your business.) You don't actually need a website to run a business like this. Of course if you plan on making this huge, it's probably a good idea to build your own website so you can capture a global clientele. Step by step please. Start with family first, the move on to the companies around you and so on.

- Have you ever heard of **PPC** (Pay Per Click)? Well, if you have experience in this, then set up a Facebook PPC campaign and again, make sure to include your contact information in your ad before you set it off, and watch your clients come running to you.

- Get ad space in your **local newspaper** if you can afford to do so. I know I said you would only spend $1/month, but hey, this is a business. You will always be expected to invest back in your own business in order to get new clients.

- Make yourself a set of beautiful looking (professional) **business cards**. Do not leave your house without them. Give them to everyone and their mother. It's free face-to-face advertising and you'll get some amazing results. People usually keep business cards, and refer back to them at some point in time. So this works both long term and short term.

This should be way more than enough to get your desired customer base. If you've read through the whole book, then you are bound to make some connections from other models. You can mix and match ideas to get your company name out there. Use social media. Do smart searches to find customers looking for specific things, etc…Be creative and good luck! No wait, scratch that. I'm not into the whole "luck" thing. Work hard and you will succeed.

35. **Number Games.** I've saved the best till last. This is quite a genius business model that has made some people multi-millionaires. I'm in the process of studying the model in great detail, but I'll explain the basics to you first and maybe if someone would like to partner with me on this, we can figure out a way to make it happen.

There's this guy (who shall remain nameless). He has an average career in stock picking. For those that don't know what that means, he basically picks stocks (in the stock market) that he thinks will either succeed tomorrow or fail. He has a tiny clientele and is not satisfied with the money he's making. He decides to try something completely out of the box.

Before I continue with this story, I would like to let you in on a marketing technique that some of you will already know about, but others, maybe not. E-mail databases. These are exactly what they sound like. Massive databases filled with your email addresses which can be filtered by categories. For example, if you once signed up for a finance newsletter, or whatever subject, your email address may end up in a massive database of email addresses which are then sold to companies who will proceed to send you emails about their products, etc...you get the point, right?

Ok, back to the story. This gentlemen decides to buy a finance database of 1,000,000 email addresses. You're probably thinking, how do I handle 1,000,000 email addresses? For starters, your Gmail account can only send 500 emails per day. You don't want to sit for the next couple of months sending 500 emails per day, you'll never finish. So he used the very popular marketing software (Aweber & Mailchimp). These two allow you to send huge amounts of marketing material via email.

He first divided the million emails into two groups. 500,000 each. Let's call these group A and group B. He sent group A an email saying that a particular stock price would go up, he then sent group B an email saying that the same stock price would go down. The next day when everyone saw the stock price go up, he dumped all the group B email addresses (because these guys saw him get it wrong). So the 500,000 people in group A have now seen him get the stock pick correct.

Now, he has 500,000 email addresses in total. He divide those into two groups of 250,000 and did the same thing. Each time getting rid of the group that was wrong. He did the following combinations:

- **Group A = 125,000 / Group B = 125,000**
- **Group A = 62,500 / Group B = 62,500**
- **Group A = 31,250 / Group B = 31,250**
- **Group A = 15,265 / Group B = 15,625**

Once he reach the 15,000 range, the group that got the correct advice have now see this guy get it right 6 or 7 times in a row and they are so impressed. They label him a guru! You won't believe what happens next. He invites the remaining 15,625 people to attend his private stock picking seminar for US$5,000/person.

A quick calculation tells us that this gentlemen earned US$78,125,000 in 6-7 days. I'm going to spell that out for you. That's seventy eight million, one hundred and twenty five thousand US dollars in the bank. Why? Because he is a genius. Thinking so far out of the box has made him almost instantly rich. This is one of the best lessons I have ever learned about making big money, fast. Yes, it requires you to do some work. Yes, he was actually a stock picker, so he put in the hard work studying finance, but I tell you, it paid off in the end.

I've spent the last few months studying every aspect of this model and I'm more and more interested, the more I discover what he went through. It's very possible to replicate, but I'm having a big issue with this possibly being SPAM. From what I've learned, you are free to send emails to anyone in the world, as long as you include the following two options at the bottom of the email:

- A link to "Unsubscribe"
- Your company address

If those two options are included, you are safe. However, I don't know what the content of his email was and how he designed it to be eye catching enough for people to take seriously. In any case, this really opened my eyes to endless possibilities and I truly hope this section of my book on making money has helped you get rid of your excuses and pushed you to start thinking of how you're going to start making money tomorrow.

11 HOW TO TAKE NOTES LIKE A SUPER NERD

Taking notes is an art form in my opinion. As an entrepreneur, you should always be on the look-out. Ideas are constantly popping off in your head every time you look at something around you. Every time you hear something interesting, your first reaction is record it somewhere. Right? Well, let me tell you how it really is. You learn something really awesome. You forget to write it down and tomorrow that potential opportunity is history. Ok, some of you will probably be thinking, "that's unfair. I always write things down". I accept that. But where do you write it down? On a small post-it sitting on your table? What happens when you need to write down more stuff? A second post-it on your table? How about that scrap piece of paper you find over there? Why not the back of the envelope that just came in the mail?

We all do this. It's our first quick reaction when we learn something new. This is similar to online bookmarking in my personal opinion. It is only useful on your browser on the computer you book marked it on (for the regular individual). Now let's take a simple scenario. 6 months pass by and for some reason or another, you need read that one sentence from that one article on that one website you visited 6 months ago. Or you need that one number you wrote on that one post-it note (you can't even remember the color of that post-it) 6 months ago. Where is that post-it note? Because when I decided to do that spring cleaning session, I think I might have chucked it with a whole bunch of old mail, which perhaps also contained some vital information I had written on the back of it. Oh snap. What to do?

Ok, I think I've rubbed it in enough and I have gone through this so many times in my life that I had to teach myself how to do all this in a more efficient and simplified manner. Please note that just consolidating the scraps into a binder is not going to get the job done if you don't know how to find it in that massive binder. We need a manual content management system, which is exactly what I'm about to show you.

I am going to split this chapter into two parts. The first part is manual note taking (i.e. writing your notes by hand). The second part will be the very many options you have when it comes to digital note taking and retrieval of those notes in an efficient manner. Let's get started:

1. Buy yourself a handy little notebook. My suggestion is to go with the Moleskine variety. They are the perfect size. They're lined and don't have page numbers. Perfect! In fact, there is a really amazing one from Evernote which I recently purchased. It looks beautiful and has some tech features embedded in it.

2. Great! Now that we've done the part that everyone in the world does, let's do something slightly different. Open up your new notebook and take the first page. Write "1" in the top right corner. Now flip that page and on the back of the same page, you're going to write "1.5" on the top left corner. Do you get it? Each page of your note book is not 2 pages. It's 1.5 pages. Continue doing that until you've done let's say, 30 pages. When you've actually filled 30 full pages of your notebook, you can then move on to filling out the next 30 pages up to 60 and so on, just so you don't get bored from the get go.

3. Fantastic! Now we've got an empty notebook with 0.5 page numbers in all the corners. Give yourself a round of applause, because believe it or not, you've just created your first manual index system. Something your computer does in seconds in the background, but now you're in control. What's next? Ok, now go to the front of your notebook and find the blank inside cover. Write "Contents Page" in beautiful handwriting, centered at the top of the page.

4. You are now ready to go. Go nuts! Take notes about everything you need. Absolutely everything. My suggestion is that you try to keep one subject on one side of a page, otherwise it can get messy. So, for example, if on page "1" I took notes for a meeting I was going to have and on page "1.5" I reviewed a chapter for class,

then I would go to my contents page and write something like this: "1" (put a circle around the number to make it easy to locate in the future) – Notes for meeting with XX Supplier on 22-JAN-2013. Under that, I would write "1.5" – Chapter 6 notes of Financial Engineering material for last semester. Remember, your contents page doesn't have to be in any specific order whatsoever! That's what's so great about this system. As long as there is a number and a small blurb describing what is available on that page, you will be able to find anything you need in less than a minute.

5. 6 months from now when you're looking for what you discussed in that meeting with so and so, or that really cool website that will help you with your business, you're going to quickly scan your contents page and locate that exact page which without this content management system would have taken you days to find, or would have been long gone on a piece of paper which you threw away with the rest of your mail.

Once you've mastered this with your first notebook, you will never stop taking notes, because you now know how to find every note you've ever taken. Remember at the beginning of this chapter, I called this an art form? Well, there is a name for this art form of excessive yet precise note taking and it's called "Hypergraphia". Heard of Dostoevsky? Well, he was a member of this elite club of super nerd note taking.

I trust a hand-written note over a digital note or my memory. No matter how scattered my notes are, I can now do the following:

- Review book highlights in under 10 minutes
- Connect all the scattered notes I took to write this book, in under 10 minutes, knowing that this would have either been an impossible feat, or would have taken me dozens of hours

With that, we conclude the first part of this chapter. We're are now manual note taking professionals. We can take notes on any subject, all in one note book, on any page and still find those exact notes 6 months later in under 10 minutes. Let's move onto the digital world, where I like to live.

We are going to look at how you can setup your computer life in a structure way, using some great tools that will help you create a "Never Forget Again" system along with some key habits required for using that system. I will share with you my personal setup as well as other tools that may interest you.

Let's begin by looking at my personal setup. I have chosen this setup because I always need a digital version of my notebook when I'm at work, or doing online research for my lifestyle experiments. Sometimes I just don't want to carry my notebook around if I don't happen to have a bag with me that day. I still need to be able to take notes quickly, easily and be able to retrieve them when my brain wants them. I need my digital life to be like my brain. When I need something, I recall it and use it on the spot, so here goes:

1. <u>Evernote</u>. A glorious app. So nicely laid out. Compatible on all devices. That's right. All devices. I have this installed on my Windows based computer at the office, on my Mac at home, on my work iPhone, on my personal Android phone and my iPad. If it's not installed on a friend's computer, I can access all my notes by simply logging into evernote.com on any web browser, and I will have all my notes in front of me for use at anytime. Now for the really cool part. You can snap photos on your phone and embed them straight into your note. I do this when I write blog posts on the go. If I'm writing about a meal I had at a restaurant, I'll snap a picture of a dish and just slide it into my note for easy access later. Another really awesome feature is when you have it installed on your computer, you can take small clips of a website and embed them into your notes. My personal favorite feature is the "audio" button. I use it in meetings and also when I'm on vacation. I like to include a small audio clip with my notes to remind me of the sounds in the area I was writing that note. The best thing is this is all FREE!

   Remember in the first part of this chapter, I mentioned the Evernote Moleskine notebook? Well get this, the Moleskine comes with digital markers which you can stick as reference points in your note book. You can then use your camera phone to take a photo of that page and it automatically gets filed in with the rest of your notes and becomes searchable, so it's the perfect way to digitize your manual note taking (if you can be bothered – I can't).

2. <u>Gmail</u>. Bet you would have never thought Gmail was a weapon in my arsenal, well it could have easily been number 1, but Evernote still has those extra features that put it just above Gmail. The archive function, mixed with labels (which you can color) along with an extremely powerful search allow me to find any email I want in a matter of seconds. All I really have to do is remember a specific word in an email I wrote a year ago, and Gmail will find all

the combinations for me in a matter of seconds! Bringing Evernote into the equation, I sometimes send my Evernote book an email from Gmail and use that as a way to take notes. So, sometimes if I have a very important email that I want to save as a note at the same time, I simply add my Evernote address in the BCC box to save even more time.

3. <u>Anxiety</u>. Although this is not accessible everywhere you go, it's very lightweight and very simple, and it sits right on my Mac. Since I don't use Outlook at home (which has a great to-do list system), I use anxiety at home to place my personal to-do items after reading my emails. It just takes a quick keystroke to do that.

4. <u>Jott</u>. The app that ties all apps. It's an ultra fast note taking app that is tied to all my other apps. For example, I could take a quick note about something and tell Jott to send that note to my Evernote book as well as to my Gmail account because I'll probably need to include that note in an email later. Wait, what if the note I just took was sort of a to-do note? Well, I just send it to Gmail, then when I get home, with a single keystroke, I add it to my Anxiety app and I'm all set. Everything is connect and I should never forget anything ever again.

Want to make all of this even faster? Download <u>Quicksilver</u> for Mac. It lets you do all the actions I mentioned above, using keyboard shortcut magic!

Yes, it all sounds so nice and simple, and it is! However, if you want to successfully manage your time and quickly retrieve your information, there are some habits you need to form, and quickly:

1. **Take notes, immediately.** Get used to taking notes as soon as you learn something new, or you think you'll need that piece of information for something else. You can even take this as far as placing your Moleskine on your bedside table just in case you wake up with an insanely cool idea! Or you just want to record what you can remember from your dreams because they make for some really great novels.

2. **Be consistent.** Make sure you create a sort of mental system for the apps you choose to make your life easier. So if use Jott to send out mini-notes to your Gmail and Evernote, then do that every day so that you become very fast at it. This system will not be so effective if you keep switching from app to app to do certain tasks.

Find what's the best way for you and stick to it.

3. **Be quick.** To help with #2, try finding the lightest (fastest) app to use while you're on the go, because this will motivate you to take more notes frequently. If you have to sit and wait for something to load before you can type a note, then you'll just end up never taking notes.

4. **No more filing.** There is no need to try and look like a smartass and make a million folders and sub-folders in your email program. Believe me, if you do that, you will never find the email you're looking for. This applies to everything else digital. Gmail's archive and search functions are magical. Use them! Just type in what you're looking for instead of trying to remember which folder your filed that email in. The only time I ever use folders in Gmail is if I get repetitive newsletters for example. I know a certain email address will send me a newsletter every week, so I program my Gmail to automatically file any email from that address into a folder so I can read them later. Other than that, I just leave my emails as they are and use the search function whenever I want. It never fails.

All of the above has been my personal setup and I know I've spent quite a bit of time going through each item (because I like them), but now I would like to give you more options. Everyone has their own style, so find yours:

Note-taking Tools

1. <u>OneNote</u>: This is the default note-taking tool for anyone who uses Microsoft Office, and it's very powerful. Unfortunately for some of us, it only runs on Windows I believe.

2. <u>Yojimbo</u>: A Mac-only program, Yojimbo is beloved by its many users for its power, flexibility, and easy of use. It's super fast to add things into Yojimbo, which is a great selling point.

3. **Backpack and Packrat**: One of the best of many web apps for collecting info, <u>Backpack</u> is versatile and easy to use. You can store notes, text, images, links and more … and send items via email and SMS text messages. It also has a calendar and reminders. For Mac OSX users, there's also a desktop application, <u>Packrat</u>, that works well with Backpack for off-line needs.

4. <u>Text files</u>: The simplest method of all — and one that I've used with success. Create a series of text files for different needs, and copy and paste your notes into the appropriate text files. I have text files for ideas, to-do items, errands, notes and shopping lists. Small and fast. Works very quickly if you use a program such as <u>Quicksilver</u> for opening the appropriate text file or even <u>adding text</u> to the end of the file without having to open it.

Email Apps

1. <u>Mail.app</u>: Mac OSX users love their Mail.app, a program that comes with Macs and that has some very powerful filters for manipulating emails and to-do items. Can sync with different computers if you use Apple's online service. **Webmail**: If you don't like Gmail, there are many other types of webmail, including <u>Yahoo</u> or <u>Hotmail</u>. I just think Gmail's the best.

2. <u>Outlook</u>: Of course, Outlook is the default mail program for PCs, and it's actually a pretty good program for capturing most of your data, including calendar and to-do items, although I won't list it in the categories below because it's already listed here.

Calendars

1. <u>iCal</u>: Free, simple, but great calendar program for Mac users.

2. <u>30 Boxes</u>: Good online program, but not as good as Google Calendar, in my opinion.

3. <u>Sunbird</u>: Open-source, cross-platform calendar app from Mozilla, the creator of Firefox.

To-do Apps

1. <u>Things</u>: Awesome Getting Things Done app for the Mac. Simple, easy to use.

2. <u>Omnifocus</u>: Another GTD program for the Mac, maybe the most powerful there is.

3. <u>iGTD</u>: Yet another great GTD program for the Mac. It's hard to choose between these three.

4. **RTM**: Remember the Milk is probably the most popular online to-do app, and it's extremely flexible — you can integrate it with Gmail, Twitter, Jott, text messages, email and more. Other good online to-do apps include Nozbe and Vitalist.

On-the-go Tools

1. **Mobile devices**: the iPhone, Blackberry and various PDAs are all good choices for capturing tasks and information on the go.

2. **Pocket notebook**: Please refer to the first part of this chapter.

And with that, I guarantee you will never again forget a thing. Everything should now be organized in a way that you just have to point and click to get the information you need, no matter how long ago you wrote it. These are just a few methods you can use to make your life easier and actually get things done. I'm sure there are another million apps that do the same, if not better, but I simply cannot collect them all.

If you do come across some really cool apps that help with everything I've mentioned, then please please please share it with me on my blog. I love learning new things, and I'll probably Jott them down in my Evernote.

12 THE ULTIMATE SOCIAL MEDIA PLAN

In this chapter, I want to share a social media blueprint that should help you with your efforts in tackling the ever changing world of social media. The consumer world today is rapidly changing. Long gone is the era of passive consumerism, these days consumers want to have their say on every product and service they invest in. And with the cutthroat competition, companies are actively seeking ways to gain more leverage through innovation. With the birth of a whole new universe of social media, businesses play an entirely different ballgame.

Is Your Business Social Enough?

Today, social media platforms have invaded and taken over public consciousness. It has become a big part of day to day routines and an indispensable communication tool for people to connect and stay in touch. Consumers have used social media presence as one of the integral basis of a company's legitimacy, reliability and viability. Businesses today are judged based on their Facebook or LinkedIn profiles, and consumers expect companies to respond to the concerns and queries they have tweeted within the day or within the hour.

Suffice it to say, social media has managed to steal the thunder away from traditional marketing methods. Modern marketing strategies today have a mix of social media tactics as its integral component for reaching business goals.

Discover the Social 5-pack

Highly competitive companies have taken the aggressive path and actively pursued the "Social 5-Pack", made up of: Facebook, Twitter, Google+, LinkedIn and YouTube. This is in line with the aim to engage their target market and existing client base in order to fill the top of the sales funnel as well as understand the prevailing consumer preferences and behaviors to ensure brand loyalty.

However, signing up and maintaining multiple accounts on all social networking sites is not as easy as it seems. Jumping right in without any in-depth understanding of the social media process can prove to be potentially detrimental for a company, which can lead to exposing its online presence at serious risk and leading it towards an unproductive direction.

Take The Reins of Your Online Presence

Given the power of social media, it is critically important for businesses to work through their strategies and develop processes to lead to scalability, efficiency, and successful social engagement. This chapter provides you with all the necessary information to understand the full potential of social media, as well as how your business can harness its latent power so you can make smarter decisions on how your organization can effectively incorporate it into your company's marketing and communications mix.

If you want to drive your business forward, you need to make sure it stays social, current and relevant in consumers' consciousness. Discover how social media can become your most effective and influential marketing workhorse. This chapter will equip you will all the important information on how to get started and how you can use social media to your full advantage and rake its long-term rewards.

Let's start of by understanding the value of Social Media buzz and what it can do for your business.

These days, social media is the buzz word in marketing and a global trend that has gotten everyone of every age engrossed in one, two and possibly even several social media sites. Everyone is on it, in one form or another. But what is it exactly?

Social Media Explained in Plain English

The term social media has been carelessly tossed around and used too often in online marketing. But what is it really about? In essence, social media incorporates the use of online technologies and methods that allow people to share personal opinions, content as well as swap insights and perspectives with the rest of the world.

Social media content can take different shapes and forms:

- Text – often used to write or put across personal opinions or posts
- Images – photos are used to display anything of interest
- Audio – podcasts can be created for other users to download
- Video – video content can be shared to engage, entertain or educate

Among the most popular social media sites at the moment include:

- Social Networking: Facebook, LinkedIn, Twitter, Google+
- Wikis: Wikipedia
- Video Sharing: YouTube
- Photo Sharing: Instagram, Pinterest, Flickr
- News Aggregation: Digg, Reddit
- Online Gaming: World of Warcraft

The New Approach to Branding and Communication – Moving Beyond Marketing

Social media has paved the way to a more powerful communication channel for companies to publish their marketing messages – all without the exorbitant cost. While we all know social networks are generally used by businesses to engage their target market and study consumer preferences and behaviors, the truth is, it has other equally powerful features that you can incorporate into your marketing strategy, with highly rewarding payoffs at that.

Here are other areas in your business that you can apply social media to drive success:

- Customer Service – One ideal example of this is Best Buy. With their Twelpforce, employees are empowered to provide prompt assistance on issues and queries. The ability to respond and react quickly is very critical in today's market, especially in influencing and changing perceptions. Even if a concern has not been resolved immediately, customers will feel their issues were acknowledged and given attention in a timely manner.

- Internal Communications and Collaboration – Small and large organizations can largely benefit from social media, in terms of file sharing, collaborative editing and knowledge sharing.

- Recruitment and Retention – A lot of employees today decide on whether they want to be a part of an organization or not based on information derived from social networks. It can also present a powerful tool in sourcing social channels that exists through professional networks.

Understanding the Social Media Ecosystem

To effectively use social media to your full advantage, it is important to take time and learn how the ecosystem works and the emerging habits of the "social consumers". Consider each social networking site as a town and the ecosystem basically pertains to the infrastructure of that town.

Your knowledge of the ecosystem will provide you a virtual map to navigate your way around the streets and how to find the path towards connecting with your target market. According to the latest study conducted by Chadwick Martin Bailey, consumers who are both Twitter followers and Facebook fans of a certain brand will not only recommend its products or services but also buy from those brands. In the same study, consumers reveal that brands that do not engage in social media are perceived as "out of touch" and outdated.

So the main idea here is to focus your social media efforts on the power users who command influence within their social networks. However, it is also important to note that connecting with medium and light users will also help your business earn social proof and trust.

Converting Leads to Sales: The ROI of Social Media

Like any business endeavor, you naturally want to have a fair idea on the return of your investment in social media and not simply jump right in just because it's the popular thing to do. The ROI cycle of social media can be separated into 3 stages:

Stage 1: The Launch

At this stage, 100% of your focus is on setting up accounts on the 5 Social Packs: Facebook, Twitter, Google+, LinkedIn and YouTube. While there are a number of other popular social networking sites, the 5 are considered to be the critically important ones. You simply can't afford not to have presence on all 5 platforms.

The Launch stage is more of an execution stage with the primary goal of getting started. Here are the details of this stage:

Approach: Execution
Objectives: Social Media Presence
Focus: Short-Term
Results: Negligible

At this point, you won't be able to expect any significant impact or derive results.

Stage 2: Management

At this stage, about 60% of your company's efforts will be focused on developing the 5 social media sites. About 10% of the focus is directed towards the creative and brand offer and 20% on setting up quantitative metrics like inbound links, traffic, Facebook "likes", etc. The remaining 10% will be focused on qualitative metrics such as survey results, pools and studying brand sentiment.

Approach: Tactical
Objectives: Customer Engagement
Focus: Mid-Term
Results: Increase in Traffic

Stage 3: Optimization

During the Optimization stage, 25% of the focus is on gaining more leverage on all 5 social media platforms, and 30% will be distributed to creative and brand offer development, as well as the quantitative and qualitative metrics. The other 25% of the focus will be directed to improving the conversion rate and the optimization of campaigns. The remaining 20% will be used to measure success of the campaign which will be the basis of your ROI.

Approach: Strategic
Objectives: Social Media ROI
Focus: Long-Term
Results: Increase in Revenue

Despite what many social experts claim, that ROI of social media cannot be measured, there is actually a way to measure it. This process will require a better understanding of your customer lifetime value (CLV) or the average revenue generated by a customer during their entire engagement period with your products and services. This figure will be used to compare the results that have been generated on your campaign in social media.

For example:

If a typical customer spends about $10 every month on a particular product and has been a loyal patron of a certain brand for about 3 years, this equates to the average customer lifetime value of $360.00.

Most companies are willing to spend about 10% of their CLV for the acquisition of new customers. This means, they are willing to spend $36 to acquire a new customer who is expected to spend $360 all throughout his/her engagement with the brand.

So if your social media efforts will cost you $36,000 for one full year, and your campaign will be able to generate 1,000 new customers every year, then you definitely have a clear winner in your hands.

Developing a Winning Social Media Marketing Plan

First, here is a quick glimpse on some revealing social media statistics:

- Facebook – According to ExactTarget, the primary reason why people "LIKE" a Facebook page is to establish a sales relationship with a specific brand, through the following: to receive promotions and coupons (40%), derive instant updates on upcoming sales (30%), and to show support for certain brands or companies (30%)

- Twitter -- According to Edison Research, 40% of the total time people are on Twitter are spent on learning about certain products and services or reading/getting feedback from what others have to say about them as well as share personal opinions and experiences.

Social Media is all About Building Relationships

As more and more companies and brands readily include their product offers in the social media experience, a growing number of consumers have grown increasingly comfortable with the idea of social commerce.

Given the promising potential of social media, it is important to have a flexible marketing strategy in place that can grow and adjust with the ever changing trend. By taking time to develop processes from both the corporate and the individual standpoint, you will be able to sustain healthy social engagement activities over time. You can do this by building communities and relationships by listening, responding and creating value.

7 Essential Steps for Creating a Successful Social Media Strategy

According to the Social Media Marketing Report for 2010, an estimated 67% of marketers have actively increased and strengthened their social media channels. As more and more companies work on integrating social media into their corporate marketing and communication plans, there is a growing emphasis for creating a winning social media strategy. Without any semblance of a plan or strategy, your presence might as well be nonexistent or muted.

But how do you exactly develop a strategy to best cater to the unique behavior and characteristics of your niche? Here is a 7-step guide to make sure you hit the ground running on your social media campaign:

First, An Important Prerequisite

If you are working for a big company or organization, before you start formulating your social media strategy, it is absolutely critical for the stakeholders of the business to believe in the potential of social media and that the primary goal is not just to simply sell products and services.

Your company should not launch a social media campaign to join the bandwagon and in response to the fact that everyone else is doing it. Social media is not a temporary marketing gimmick or project with an expiry date, but a long-term commitment with invaluable benefits. It is important for organizations to recognize that constant testing and experimentation are required every so often to study the effectiveness.

Now that we have that covered, here are the 7 critically important steps to guide you through developing your very own social media strategy:

1. **Define Your Goals and Objectives.** Determine what are your specific social media objectives and goals and how they complement and support the overall goals of the company.
2. **Research, Research and More Research.** Don't make the mistake of simply jumping in with a sea of competition and discerning consumers without having any clue. Research is very important as basis for execution. This will include the action plan for the 5 major social media platforms. Take time to check out what's out there, scope the competition and understand your target audience.
3. **Prepare a Database of Contacts and Content.** If you go about your social media campaign correctly, social relationships will start to develop naturally. Start establishing connections by following conversations relevant to your branding. Make a list that will identify the key influencers and power users that play an important role in your industry.
4. **Join Conversations to Start Developing and Forging Relationships.** Start answering questions relevant to your industry, give your opinion and join a community. This will not only help you start your network, it will also help you build your reputation as an industry expert and a thought leader.

5. **Strengthen Your Social Media Relationships.** Don't just hide behind an avatar or brand, make your presence known by attending events that encourage face-to-face interactions. This includes offline events that are relevant to your industry.
6. **Take Time to Measure Results.** You have already established your goals and objectives, right? It is equally important to measure your success. Among the most common goals include:

   1. Enhance brand presence across social media platforms
   2. Increase traffic to company website
   3. Increase positive consumer sentiment and perception towards brand
   4. Develop relationships for potential partnership opportunities in the future

7. **Analyze, Adjust and Improve.** Once you have measured your success and progress towards your goal, you need to analyze and identify key areas that need improvement, adapt to changing trends and improve your overall social media campaign. Remember, it is not always a straight road ahead, so you need to constantly evaluate and adjust.

The Golden Rules of Social media

Social media is very complex and a constantly evolving medium. It's no wonder why many businesses struggle to figure it out and keep up. While a number have enjoyed quantifiable success, there are also many who failed, and the rest have still yet to figure out their social media strategy.

Failure is often brought about by overlooking the importance of understanding the concept of social media. The very basic question as to "why people engage in it?" as well as "what are the unwritten rules governing it?" While it is true that social media gives businesses free exposure, many organizations fail to carefully plan the message they want to convey, as they would have normally done for any expensive ad campaign.

Consider this: In the joint study conducted by Facebook and Nielsen back in 2010, the report revealed that the following benchmarks are used on social media for enterprise: brand awareness, ad recall and purchase intent. It is not surprising to note that in the study, it was found out that social media has been able to generate significantly far better results than traditional marketing approaches and campaigns.

Much like dating, any organization needs to woo, nurture and meet the needs of their network. To help you out, below are the following rules that apply to any type of social media user, whether individual, business or non-profit. If you seriously want to harness a powerful platform to propel your business, acquire new clients, increase sales as well as enhance brand awareness, here are the golden rules you should abide by and respect:

- **Social media is all about building relationships, not business transactions.** Any attempt to overtly sell a certain product or service can easily damage your online presence. Consumers no longer have to think of excuses and come up with a polite "no" to a persuasive sales person, all they have to do is to click the "unfollow" button. Don't make the blunder of using an autoresponder to thank individuals who decided to follow you on Twitter.

- **Organizations must assign a dedicated social media expert.** Don't make the mistake of assigning anyone to handle your social media campaign. The person must be qualified and work independently as a social media evangelist and report directly to top executives.

- **Organizations should focus on cultivating engagement and not on figures.** The number of followers, likes and the size of network should not be considered as a performance indicator. There is greater value in maintaining a smaller network with regular interactions and active engagements.

- **Define your target audience and identify specific area of expertise.** Don't try to cater everyone by being all things to all people. If you are truly keen to reaching power users, key decision makers and influencers, your content should be designed around your market.

- **Content still reigns supreme in social media.** As stated, social media is not a place to publish your award-winning sales pitches. Posts should be clear and concise, not emotional or impulsive. It should be carefully constructed and always politically correct. Twitter posts in particular should be free from any gimmicks or hidden strings attached but instead provide information, free resources and best practices.

- **Updates should be frequent and consistent.** Social media campaigns are long-term and ongoing efforts, and work as an integral part of the company's online presence. It is not a 9 to 6 weekday job. It is generally best for posts and updates to be published daily, no more than 7 to 9 times.

- **Social media platforms should be manifested.** All social media streams and accounts should be linked to all pages of the website, include all the "like", "follow" and "tweet" buttons.
- **Social media profiles MUST be impeccable.** Profiles are the first and most viewed page in social media platforms. But all too often, it is the most ignored aspect. All elements, including background, images and messages should be consistent with the corporate image and brand.

Setup and Manage a Facebook Page That Works

Facebook is perhaps the most famous global phenomenon that continues to grow exponentially since its launch. Originally designed for college students, we don't need statistics to prove that Facebook has moved leaps and bounds beyond its original use. Over time, it is recognized as an extremely powerful networking medium for businesses.

What is it?

Facebook is a type of social networking service launched way back in February 2004, and is operated by Facebook, Inc. Recent reports as of February 2012, Facebook has reached an astonishing 845 million active users. To use its services, users need to register and create profiles, exchange messages, post statuses, upload photos, chat with friends and so much more. From a simple social medium it has evolved into a widely popular professional networking site.

Why use it?

- **Great Exposure.** With millions of users, Facebook offers unrivalled potential for exposure. When used strategically and consistently, Facebook can contribute to the significant increase in your company's online presence and visibility. Post comments, provide insights, advice and tips to earn respect and credibility in your network, and ultimately gain leverage.
- **Improve Google Rank.** With Facebook's "Pages" application, you can create a professional profile for products, services and business. Within these pages, you are provided with the option to include links to your website and "like" buttons. This helps drive traffic towards your website and generate more interest.
- **Powerful Marketing Platform for Free.** Facebook use, as you already know is absolutely free of charge. It allows you to reach out

to hundreds, even thousands of people with a host of user-friendly applications and tools you can use to market products and services.

- **Targeted AD Space.** For a reasonable fee, you can also create ads and target them to reach specific gender, location and age group, as well as track its performance.
- **Provide Regular Updates.** Facebook offers you a convenient way to update your network on new products, promotions, and general information about your company to stay fresh and relevant in the minds of your market.
- **Facilitate Online Discussions to Gain Valuable Inputs.** Use newsgroups and networks as a venue to discuss, and respond to comments and inquiries. It can also be a great source of constructive feedback to help you enhance your products or services.
- **Stay Connected and Nurture Relationships.** Provide useful information to your fans and network on a regular basis. This includes helpful how-to videos and other relevant content which your market may enjoy.
- **Enhance Customer Service.** Consumers these days prefer real-time response to queries and concerns. The Facebook page for your business offers a convenient and accessible option for your market to reach you.

Setting Up

Creating a Facebook Page (also known as Brand Page) can provide you a powerful tool to interact with your market on a different level that traditional media will not be able to provide. By helping your customers gain a close connection with your corporate brand, you can turn them into loyal patrons and unpaid brand ambassadors.

To get started, follow these simple steps:

1. If you don't have an existing account, sign up for one. If you already have one, log in and click "Pages" button located on the left-hand side of the screen.
2. Select what type of Facebook page you want to create, such as Brand, Company, Institution and Organization.
3. Fill in all the specific information.
4. Agree to the detailed Facebook Pages Terms.
5. Enter all the relevant information required. Once you have indicated the specific category of your business, you can start customizing

your page. Facebook walks you through the entire customization process by providing you a list of pending things you should complete to get started.

6. Upload a company image or logo, which you can also include website, tagline, and Twitter page, along with other social media pages you maintain.
7. Save your settings.

Configuring and Optimizing

- **Add content.** Include key information such as website links, location, business hours, and photos/products/menus so people will have a general idea what your business is all about. Focus on providing brief but engaging information under Info tab. Think SEO and use keywords since each tab can be indexed by search engines.

Power Tip: If you will key in your website URL starting with http:// in the info box right under the profile picture, Facebook will automatically turn it into a clickable link. This will allow you to conveniently refer visitors to your website, twitter account or company blog.

- Claim your place. Connect your Facebook Page to your physical store location people can find you as well as check in.
- Invite your customers. Invite current customers to like your page. You can send out newsletters, advertise in your website, post links, or promote in-store through flyers, etc.

Power Tip: The efficient way to set up your Facebook Page and add existing clients is to create a separate Gmail account for your Facebook account. Import the email addresses of your clients there. When you create your Facebook Page, the system will automatically find your clients from your address book and suggest them as your friends.

- **Add the "LIKE" button to your website**. To effectively promote your Facebook page, add the like button in your website and blogs so people can engage with your Page as well as share it with their own network.

Engage Your Customers

- **Interact and join conversations**. Maximize visibility and presence by posting regular updates on your wall about your business. You can also provide exclusive offers that will generate interest and comments and drive active engagement.
- **Build deeper relationships**. Use this opportunity to get to know your loyal client base or "fans" and go out of your way to make them feel at home by responding to comments in a timely manner.
- **Gain valuable insights**. Learn and study how your audience interact and make the necessary adjustments to increase and encouragement more engagement.

Promote Your Business

- **Create Ads.** Make use of Facebook Ads to promote your business and get the word out based on your targeted criteria like location, interest, age group, etc.
- **Run Sponsored Stories.** Set up Sponsored Stories, so you can encourage friends/fans to spread the good word about your business to their network. Remember, word of mouth marketing is twice as effective when it comes to driving results compared to traditional advertising.

Stand Out From The Crowd

- **Get a vanity URL.** Instead of the unappealing ""3267783386?ref=sg&ajaxpe=1&_a=7" URL, customize it into something professional, like http://facebook.com/mybusiness name. To be able to do this, you need to have at least 25 fans.
- **Customize landing page.** To stand out, you need to have an attractive and striking landing page, which can significantly help visitors become fans of your page.

Power Tip: If you don't have access to web design skills, you can purchase a Facebook template from templates stores.

90

More Tips on Promoting Your Facebook Page

1. Using your social media Manager:

- Actively add people that can potentially become customers or those who related to your specific line of business.
- Use the Search function to discover relevant or related pages, events, people, groups and even messages. This can also be used to keep track of any brand mentions as well as provide timely feedback.
- Communicate. It's an interactive page, so make sure to answer back.

Power Tip: When you are composing a post or message, put an @ sign and type in your business page so you can mention it. You can even use this as a signature for your regular updates.

2. Cheat a little.

Ask employees and fellow staff members to post comments and "likes" on your status updates in order to boost rankings. Status updates that has 5 or more comments and "likes" can show up in the Top News section. This will also help make your Facebook wall more alive and inspire fans to participate in conversations and be more active.

3. Fill your Page with media content

- Encourage fans to post photos of how they use your products and/or services
- Upload photos of your products and/or services, including your team and office so fans can easily relate to you.
- Upload photos of events you hosted and tag your fans
- Post videos that features any of your team member's talks
- Use video to respond and entertain your fans
- Show your products and/or services in action

4. Treat your fans.

It is important to reward your fans with special or exclusive offers every now and then. You can reward loyalty by offering discounts limited only to Facebook fans.

5. Keep your fans updated.

Direct messages are very powerful, but make sure not to abuse it. Before you send messages to your fans, think twice. Your updates should be valuable and a welcome news since your goal is to inform and engage and not irritate.

6. Ask your fans for help.

Seek help from your fans in building your community using "Suggest to Friends" and "Share" tools.

7. Build partnerships with other Facebook pages.

Each page on Facebook feature a function called "Add to my Page's Favorites" button. Any "favourited" page will have their logo displayed in the "Favorite Pages" featured on your Facebook page.

8. Use applications.

There are some really useful apps on Facebook that you can readily use to promote your company or brand. You can conduct polls, quizzes, and games where people can play against each other and outrank. There are even apps for giveaways and sweepstakes – something most consumers love to participate in.

9. Spy!

Yes, you also need to keep an eye on your competitors, most especially those that are highly successful in their own campaigns. Check out what they are doing every now and then and study their strategies. If you choose to copy, make sure you offer the better version.

10. Blackhat Techniques

You didn't hear this from me, but you know it happens. I know it happens and the biggest companies in the world are doing it, so I have to mention it. Lots of people are either buying Facebook "LIKES", or are taking part in link wheels which I have mentioned in an earlier chapter. You do some work and in return, people like your Facebook page. Just be careful you don't get banned.

Tweet Your Way to Online Prominence

Twitter's simple question: "What are you doing?" has certainly generated a lot of response since its launch. From teenagers, to professionals, celebrities, politicians, corporate bigwigs – you name it, everyone is on Twitter. With the quick and frequent exchange of ideas, opinions, answers, Twitter has created a whole new universe for people from different social backgrounds, status and interest to stay connected through a more open line of communication.

Understanding the Twitter Phenomenon

What is Twitter? This is another popular social networking and micro blogging service that allows its users to send and read text-based posts or "tweets" of up to 140 characters. Twitter was created by Jack Dorsey back in March 2006 and was officially launched in July of the same year. Since then, the service has gained worldwide popularity and currently has 300 million users, generating more than 300 million tweets as well as handling more than 1.6 billion search queries every single day. Twitter has been described as the "SMS of the Internet".

Twitter offers a combination of different forms of communication -- text, photos, music, videos –evolving from everyday life experiences to interesting content, newsworthy events and crisis. Conversations can revolve on hot topics using hashtags and users can post and view updates, follow other users as well as send public replies or private messages to connect and communicate with other users. Over the years, the Twitter ecosystem has grown dramatically, enabling users to search for people, news or subjects.

Why Use it?

- **Connect with your customers**. This is the primary reason why you should make use of twitter for your business. Twitter has become so much a part of everyone's daily routine, it's the perfect venue to connect, interact, and study your target marker. **Branding**. In Twitter, you don't have to be in the league of Nike, Dell or Starbucks to brand and generate interest. In fact, it presents the best platform for small businesses and startups to reach their target niche.
- **Customer feedback**. If any customer is dissatisfied with a certain product or service, he/she will no doubt tweet about it. In this

sense, Twitter is a reliable resource to derive feedbacks and opinions, as well as study consumer behaviors and preferences.

- **Marketing.** With its wide reach, you can use Twitter to market products and/or services to a wider market and the best part is, it's free.

- **News**. Twitter is the best and fastest way to publish latest updates about your company – without the need to compose long, elaborate content.

- **Marketing schemes and promotions.** If you have existing promos and exclusive deals, let your network know about it. Everyone loves a good deal. In fact, a lot of companies have conducted contests and promos exclusively for their Twitter followers to engage their market.

- **Twitter is viral.** Once you have managed to gain a degree of popularity, you will discover how viral it can be. This can become a strategic edge for your marketing campaigns.

- **Spy on the competition**. You don't just gain insights on customers and target market, you can also read and study what the competition is doing, what are their weaknesses based on complaints and work on positioning yourself to provide a better alternative.

- **Increase sales**. Yes, Twitter can significantly help in increasing sales. According to a report published by Mashable, Dell has raked in a whopping $6.5 in sales through Twitter.

- **Brand loyalty**. In any business, you want to aim for long-term use of your products and/or services instead of one-time purchases. By engaging your clients and providing prompt value-added service, you will be able to retain customers and enjoy loyal patronage.

- **Networker's paradise**. Connect with industry leaders, the movers and shakers and influential personalities relevant to the industry you operate in. If you have attended networking events in the past and have enjoyed decent results for your company, just imagine what Twitter can do for you.

- **Generate website traffic**. When done perfectly, Twitter can be a great and effective tool to generate more interest and attract targeted market to visit your website or blog which can translate to sales leads, and ultimately convert to sales.

- **Though Leadership**. Twitter is a perfect venue to showcase your skills and expertise and provide sound advice, opinions and help resolve problems to gain more credibility as a thought leader.

How to Build And Attract Followers

As you might have already guessed, Twitter has become an indispensable social media tool to drive your business forward. It is not your typical fly by night trend that will eventually disappear into oblivion. Since its launch, it is still in its upswing. To be able to take full advantage of the full potential of Twitter, you need to carefully plan out your strategies.

Getting Started

1. **Conduct an initial search**. Create your Twitter account and use the Twitter search to check out the buzz about your name or brand, your direct competitors and other relevant words that relate to your company, products and/or services.
2. **Add a photo**. It's unappealing to interact with anyone without any photo. If you have established decent brand recognition, you can use your logo, or if you are a startup or a small organization, it is generally best to use a personal photo.
3. **Start joining conversations and talk to people about their interest**. This will convey a more personalized appeal that shows the human side behind a brand, product or service. (@wholefoods does this quite well)
4. **Generate interest**. Post interesting things that relate to your industry, and not just about your company, products or services. This can include latest news, policies, and developments, among others.
5. **Entertain to engage**. Share interesting and fascinating links that will entertain and spur interest.
6. **Use a proactive approach**. When handling complaints, don't get stuck on the vicious cycle of apologizing. Instead be helpful and offer immediate resolution, tips and guidelines. (@jetblue does this quite well by providing travel tips and advisories)
7. **Say no to blatant marketing**. Don't make the mistake of overselling your products and/or services. Others will either tune you out or hit the "unfollow" button.
8. **Become more human**. Promote interesting outside of work stories of your employees and major stakeholders. (@TheHomeDepot does this quite well)
9. **Introduce personalities**. Add in a few personalities to work along with the brand, such as RichardAtDELL, MaxeneAtDELL, etc.
10. **Really communicate**. Take time to also talk about non-business topics too.

What to Tweet About

- Instead of answering Twitters question, "What are you doing?" you can choose to answer the question, "What has caught your attention?"
- Aside from a business Twitter account, have other Twitter users in your company. People can quit, take vacations, etc.
- When promoting a particular blog post, don't just dump the link. You can either ask a question or explains what's coming up next.
- Ask questions and encourage your followers to share their opinions.
- Follow interesting and popular people. If you come across users who tweets interesting things, check out who he/she follows and follow them as well.
- Tweet about other people instead of simply focusing on you, your company, your brands or products. Twitter is not for selling and it has a more intrinsic impact on your business. Work on giving a face or personality behind a brand to engage your followers.
- When you happen to talk about your company, products or services, make sure it's useful. You can deliver it in a form, of advice, pictures, blog posts that offer insightful content.
- Don't flood timelines and tweet too much. It may easily annoy followers. As a general rule of the thumb, tweet at least 8 times in a day and no more than 15 times.
- Visit my blog (www.ramiel-ashi.co.nr) to learn how I use Twitter to maximize my reach.

More Practical Tips

- You don't have to read every single tweet.
- You don't have to reply to every single @ tweet that has been directed to you.
- Choose direct messaging options if exchanges with other people do not have value to other Twitter followers.
- Regularly check out Twitter search function to find out if there are people talking about you, your brand, company, products and services.
- One great way to build community in Twitter is to respond to tweets as well as retweet other user's posts.

Power Tips

- Post some good, intelligent tweets before following anyone.
- Complete your profile information.
- Add Twitter feed to other social media profiles and blogs.
- Reply to people who are following you, and most especially to those who don't.

Creating your Twitter account is just the start of your journey. To get the best results, Twitter, along with other social media platform should be an ongoing thing.

Build Your Network With Linkedin

Most people use LinkedIn in order to "link to someone" to form a partnership, make a sale, or get a job. Given its continuing success, it works quite well to that many professions from rank and file, to consultants, CEO and business magnates maintain an account, representing 130 different industries across the globe. However, to date, LinkedIn still remains an underutilized tool as many of its users have not fully explored its full potential and maximize its benefits.

What is Linkedin?

LinkedIn was launched back in 2003 and since then it has become the world's largest and most popular professional networking site. An estimated 1 million new members join this social media platform every week. People generally connect on LinkedIn with people that they personally or professionally know. However, unlike Facebook and Twitter, LinkedIn is perceived to be more business focused.

LinkedIn presents a great venue for its users to make or establish second or third-degree introductions and connections, which can be useful when trying to grow a business or when looking for a job, recruiting talent or seeking other employment opportunities.

To date, LinkedIn maintains over 85 million members across more than 200 countries, which includes top executives from almost every Fortune 500 companies.

Why Use it?

- **Increase visibility.** By establishing connections, you also increase your exposure and visibility. Whether you offer a product or service or both, you profile may be made available to people interested to doing business with, forge partnerships or hire services.

- **Improve network.** Connect with people from past acquaintances, people from your school, past companies, affiliations, and those who share your passions and interests.

- **Improve Google PageRank**. LinkedIn allows its users to publish and make their profile information available for search engines to index. LinkedIn profiles rank high in Google, so it's a great and effective way to influence other people's perception when they search for you.

- **Enhance search engine results**. Aside from your personal profile, you can promote your company website and blog to search engines through your LinkedIn account through the pre-selected categories such as "My Website" and "My Company".

- **Scope out the competition, partners and customers**. LinkedIn is one perfect way to keep tabs on your competition as well as partners and customers.

- **Highlight recommendations and reviews**. LinkedIn is more like a living, breathing resume of professionals that comes complete with recommendation from people you have worked with and worked for in the past. This presents a wonderful opportunity to secure business reviews as well as the specific products and services you offer.

Getting Started on Linkedin

Some people associate LinkedIn as a go-to platform for people seeking employment. It is certainly more than that. It is a great way to build portfolio and reputation, as well as connect with like-minded individuals to promote tour brand, products or services. To get started, here are some basic guidelines:

1. Enter your basic information.

2. Select "Join Now" after which you will be redirected to a second screen where you enter your personal information including professional status, company, job title, location, including pertinent information such as websites and other social media accounts.

3. Select "Create My profile". You will then be given an opportunity to search for people you already know based on your email contacts.

Customizing Your Account

When it comes to ensuring the effectiveness of your LinkedIn Page, relevance is key to establishing and maintaining strong connections. You will want to take time to customize your LinkedIn profile for a number of reasons. Social media accounts for business should be created in line with the business purpose in mind.

When creating your profile, you want to attract a particular audience. If you will check out the profiles of CFOs and compare it with community managers, you will immediately recognize the difference. So when customizing your LinkedIn profile, make sure to keep your target audience in mind.

Here are the areas you need to customize:

- **Summary.** This section should showcase you skills, assets and expertise in three to five short paragraphs. Create content that will grab attention and generate interest on the exceptional highlights of your professional career. Highlight achievements and specialties using concise words. You can use bullet points to make it more readable and drive more emphasis.
- **Professional Headline.** This appears similar to the description you have indicated in your "Current Position" unless you change it. This one appears below your name.
- **Add a Photo.** If you have other social networking accounts, you probably don't accept connections with people who don't display their profile photos, right? The same applies with LinkedIn accounts. Make sure to choose a close up headshot photo that best represents you professionally. Remember, you are your own brand, so make sure your photo demonstrates that. If you are an executive, a photo with a shirt and a cap somehow doesn't add up.

- **Experience/Work History.** Since LinkedIn is a professional networking site, make sure to highlight your best work experiences. This is an opportunity to showcase your successes. While you are not limited with the number of words you can use, make sure to keep it concise so you won't lose the attention of your audience. To guide you, here are some of the important elements you should include:

  1. List of completed projects
  2. Highlights of your position's successes
  3. Describe your strengths
  4. List down all your accomplishments and not your responsibilities
  5. If possible, include monetary benefits of your expertise and efforts, especially if you are in marketing, sales or business development

- **Recommendations.** Allow others rave about your character and capabilities with recommendations or through endorsements. You have the ability to approve and manage your recommendations so be sure to only approve the positive feedbacks. If you don't have any endorsements, you can ask someone, like a colleague, happy client or past employer.
- **Skills.** What is it that you do that's different? Your personal skills are those that make your marketable.
- **Certifications, Licenses and Accreditations.** Make sure to take time and fill this section as this can help validate your capabilities and expertise.
- **Publications.** If you have written works that has been published, include a brief description and a URL.

How to Get The Most Out of Your Linkedin Connections

After you have established your network, it's time to make sure your connections work for you. Here are some helpful tips:

1. **Ask and answer questions.** While you are signed up, you will be able to see a list of questions posted by anyone in your own extended network. Participate in these exchanges to build your reputation and gain more trust. It is also a good idea to ask questions.

2. **Recommend your colleagues.** In LinkedIn, recommendations work as a primary form of currency. Make recommendations for people you have had good experiences with. They will naturally return the favor.

3. **Learn more about your network.** Study the people within your network by reading their profiles. This can be a great basis for discussion and a foundation to build relationships on.

Expanding Your Circle With Google +

Before its launch, there have been a lot of talks generated by Google+, mostly because it is from Google itself, the kind in search engine. Since then it has become an integral part of many social media campaigns.

What is Google +?

Google+ is a social layer or network launched by Google back in July 2011 for limited testing. Users are able to configure and create circles to categorize people they are connected with into different groups, as a way of reproducing their real-life relationships.

Google+ has a number of cutting edge features, which include Hangouts, which is a multi-person video chat. Users can start a Hangout with any of existing Circles. Another great feature is Sparks, which basically enables a user to locate specific items of interest based on web-based topics.

Several months after it's launched, Google+ was able to amass 40 million registered users, which is almost one third that of LinkedIn's 135 million members. Despite its growth, it is far from surpassing Facebook, but the figures are certainly not to be ignored.

Why Use it?

- **Free SEO Boost.** Businesses can use search referrals for conversions. Google+ is built to influence search for people who have included a certain business in their Circle. This offers a great opportunity to get free promotion from people who like and use the product to people who share similar interests.

- **Host Hangouts.** The powerful chat function presents a great opportunity for businesses in engaging their customers and thought leaders in a more personal way. In addition, companies that operate from multiple locations can conveniently collaborate and share information and files such as spreadsheets and documents.

- **Expand Distribution of Content.** Google+ is a great platform to expand the publication of content distribution. It can be a great way tool to hosts contest and giveaways along with other promotions.
- **Connect with Tech-Savvy Audience.** People who are in Google+ are the "early adopters" of new technologies, a criterion which presents an ideal target market for many businesses.
- **Segment Your Audience.** One great advantage of Google+ is the option to share content with specific audiences through Circles. This makes it easier for businesses to segment their market and share content to certain followers.
- **Expand Your Network.** Be able to gather data and research on relevant contacts like potential clients and influential personalities in the industry.

Getting Started

1. **Optimize Your Page**. As stated, one of the most powerful features of Google+ is the Google search function so if you will want to make sure your page can be easily found in both regular search engine and internal search. Perform the following:

    - **Verify page with Google.** Unlike Twitter that requires a unique handle, there can be a number of pages that may have similar name as yours. Google has provided a way to verify the page to be the "official" page for a specific brand, which will be given top priority in search rankings.
    - **Add a subtitle.** Google+ allows you to place a tag line or subtitle under your brand name, with only the first 10 words visible in the header section and 21 characters are shown in pop-ups when users mouser over your page. So make sure to keep this in mind when creating your subtitle.
    - **Write a compelling introduction.** This is the prime spot on your page so make sure to use SEO-rich keywords that can be easily indexed at the same time you also need to make sure it conveys the image and message you have in mind to your audience.

2. **Upgrade the Visual Appeal of Your Page.** Make the right first impression every time people come to visit your page. You need to grab their attention and interest enough to prompt them to click and add you to their Circles.

   - Maximize the creative use of Scrapbook photos
   - Take advantage of rich-text editor

3. **Post with Quality Content**. Before you even have your first follower, you need to have at least 3 to 4 posts since this can help enhance first real impression. Perform the following for your posts:

   - Use formatting options to create posts that will look like blog posts.
   - Use videos and photos.

4. **Start Attracting Followers.** Now that you have optimized your page, you can now open your Google business page for business. Hit the ground running by performing the following:

   - Promote your page using other social media channels
   - Promote your Google page on your website
   - Post content on a regular basis
   - Follow back anyone who Circle you
   - Create VIP circles and engagers
   - Regularly monitor your comments and streams

Your Google+ profile will influence the way people will perceive your brand so make sure you give it as much attention as with the other social media platforms you maintain.

Captivate Your Audience With YouTube

While YouTube is widely popular as a form of entertainment, don't make the mistake of overlooking its significant benefits. It is more than just posting music videos, memorable moments and embarrassing events, as it is originally made popular.

More and more businesses and professionals have recognized YouTube as a powerful platform to launch themselves into stardom. While your business may not gain the same global popularity and overnight success of Justin Beiber, your business will be able to generate a good amount of interest. How? You can use videos to show off your expertise and share knowledge as well as market your products and connect with prospects, customers and colleagues.

What is YouTube?

YouTube is a web-based service that allows its users to post video files and share it with the rest of the world. Founded by the authors behind equally successful Paypal, the very first public version was released in November 2005. Since then, its popularity steadily grew and by the first quarter of 2006, it hosted 65,000 video files. By 2007, YouTube was recognized as the website with the highest amount of traffic that any other site on the web. In October of 2006, it was acquired by Google in the tune of $1.6 billion. This is considered a very viable deal since YouTube's advertising returns is reported to rake in$ 200 million every year. At this time, YouTube is enjoying millions of visits from all other the world daily.

Why Use it?

YouTube offers a cost-effective marketing platform for businesses. It is to date the cheapest form of advertising channel. Companies from various industries are using web videos as part of their marketing content to reach out to current as well as potential customers. It is now used as a way to build relationships with client base and reap its lucrative benefits as an indirect marketing strategy.

You can use YouTube with the three main goals:
- Inform
- Educate

- Entertain

Here are some ideas on how you can gain better leverage using YouTube:

Thought Leadership And Expertise

- Upload video recordings of corporate presentations to demonstrate industry authority and enhance credibility.
- Share slideshows for marketing and advertising purposes
- Conduct interviews with your own experts
- Convert podcasts into videos
- Engage with the online community of YouTube by uploading recorded video responses on specific topics relevant to your business or industry
- Record corporate meetings to share to stakeholders
- Provide presentation on upcoming products and features

Marketing And Advertising

- Put together a video that best showcase and explains your product or service
- Promote your brand using previous events
- Introduce some of the people working behind your brand to enhance authenticity
- Promote your products and services
- Post links of your videos to other social media platforms
- Run a contest
- Add call-to-action overlays to drive traffic to your corporate website
- Display company information including name, website URL, email address and phone number

Customer Service

- Create how-to videos to educate costumers on the use of your products and services
- Answers frequently asked questions using videos
- Post solutions to common service or product problems
- Embed video files to your site and blog

How to Maximize YouTube For Your Business

1. **Good content**. To ensure effectiveness and impact, you want to convey important and accurate information in the most engaging manner so other people will also want to share it to their network

2. **Plan ahead.** Make sure you have a clear idea and vision of what you want to achieve in making the video and what you want to derive from it.

3. **Avoid blatant marketing.** Resist the urge to simply put up your commercial and leave it to do its magic. Keep in mind that people don't visit YouTube to watch commercials, so you need to use a more subtle approach and soft sell by providing information in an entertaining and engaging way.

4. **Ensure high quality production.** Your videos reflect your company so make sure it's of good quality.

5. **Keep it short.** Audiences on YouTube generally have short attention span, so make sure to keep it no less that 2 to 3 minutes. If you have larger topics, cut it into segments.

Optimizing Your YouTube Videos

- Display links of your video in all your social media platforms include your main site, and blog, Facebook and Google+ page, tweet it and include them in your LinkedIn profiles.

- Focus on SEO by optimizing text descriptions with keywords and backlinks to your corporate website.

- Consider buying ads on YouTube if you have the budget. You can purchase specific videos so your video will be among the first results when users will perform a search using that keyword.

A lot of celebrities and companies have successfully generated global interest and fame by using YouTube as their launching pad. Gain strategic edge over your competition in a more creative and engaging way.

Conclusion

There is no longer a question on the power of social media in driving all types of businesses forward. No matter what type of industry you operate in, you will find that there are far too important benefits to be ignored. With the full understanding of the abilities of each social media and complete guidelines on how to best use them to your advantage, it is now up to you on how you can fully maximize its benefits for your business.

13 Reputation Management

A while back, I discussed a business model with regards to Reputation Management. I did not fully release it and ended up taking it down. So now that it has been completed, I thought I'd share it with you. You can treat this completely as a stand-alone business. You can live happily on this business model alone, but it will require you to work.

What we will be doing is, offering offline businesses an online service. Remember, then number 1 problem with people attempting to start Internet Marketing is not with "what" they want to do, but "how" they're going to do it. The purpose of this book is to answer the "how", so let's get to it.

I have personally attempted this method and these are my results. I chose to do this via Snail Mail (regular post, not email). It took me a total of 4 hours to execute. It cost me $38.94 and in return I put $17,000 in my pocket (profit). I was offered a full time job in the process (which I refused, simply because they won't pay $17,000 for 4 hours work). Remember, I do not follow through on most of my experiments. I have a full time job, but I love experimenting, and making money while experimenting is just the entrepreneurial icing on my cake.

During this campaign, I contacted a total of 22 business owners. 5 of them called me directly. I met 3 of them and closed all 3. For those don't understand the term "closed", it means I managed to convince them to sign a contract and do business with me.

Ok, let me give you a quick back story. A friend of mine was talking to me about his restaurant and how he would be getting negative reviews on his Google Places page and his Trip Advisor page, but at the same time, he would be getting compliments verbally. He blurted out a term which I knew I had to study. "Reputation Management".

I allocated a month of my life to educate myself about the ins and outs of Reputation Management. I knew if I want to pursue this experiment and succeed, I'd have to know everything about this. I had to know the figures involved and how I was going to use it to my benefit.

So, now I'm equipped with the knowledge and weapons to pitch my idea. So, I pitched a few existing clients and they ate it up like a fat kid loves cake. I decided that this could easily be put up as a stand-alone service under my existing company.

Wait wait, you're probably wondering what Reputation Management is, right? Well, I'll make it nice and simple. It is managing someone's reputation. You see what I did there? I switched the words around. Honestly, I don't know how to make it any more simple. You are literally going to manage a client's online reputation. What people are saying about your client.

To get started, I knew I that I'd need to use snail mail for this campaign because I would be putting in the hard work before starting, so I had to ensure that my efforts would at least result in my potential client reading a physical letter. Emails are just way too easy to delete without reading. My second reason being that I could personalize every aspect of my initial contact.

For the sake of this chapter, let us call this Online Reputation Management (ORM). It's a fancy term for a relatively easy job. The way you sell this service is equally as easy. You tell your potential clients "this is costing you money" and they buckle. Their ears open up and eyes are wide open (long enough for you to pitch your solution).

Because of this, ORM allows you to go nuts with your pricing. You are solving their problems after all, and you deserve to get paid for that. Some much bigger ORM companies will charge a small fortune for this service. Why not you? Obviously you will start this off as a one-man-show, but if you wish to expand your operations, you are looking at a million dollar business here.

The first question we need to answer is who are your potential prospects and where do you find them?

Start off by opening Google Maps and Notepad (you know, that thing you take notes on). Just for your information, most ORM companies will skip this manual step and head to a website called www.ripoffreport.com and will hit the F5 key all day looking for owner's who have been ripped off and approach them. In my opinion this is disgusting and is not very easy to market.

Ok, so now that we're at Google Maps, we want to look for businesses with high lifetime customer value. E.g. Restaurants, Hotels, Doctors, etc…but we need to find the ones with poor ratings. The lower the rating, the easier it will be for you to convince them that they need your service.

To start off, I suggest that you pick a specific niche and start covering all of those before moving onto a separate niche. When you find these poor reviews, jot them down in notepad (at least half a dozen). Now head over to www.manta.com and find out who the owner is and his/her address (free).

Awesome! Now we know exactly where to send our snail mail. The next obvious step is to write our beautifully worded letter that is going to catch their attention. Whatever you do, do not copy and paste the content of the letter I'm about to share with you, why? It's not because I don't want you to succeed, but imagine this: every person who reads this book and decides to give this model a shot using the same letter. Depending on the cities/countries you all live in, there will be a clash somewhere, where a business owner will get the same exact offer from two different people. That basically means you've ruined an entire region, because the business owner will feel as if something fishy is going on.

So, I advise you to take my letter. Read once or twice. Understand what is being said and re-write it in your own words to match your style. Here's my letter:

February 4, 2013
Contact name
Business Name
Business Street
City State 00000

Dear {Name},

I'm going to get straight to the point because I know you're busy; attached are some unfavorable reviews about your {business type} that I pulled from the very 1st page of Google.

My name is {Your Name}, and I'm a online reputation management consultant right here in {City, State}. I may have even been in your business at one time or even worked with some businesses near yours.

Here's the Deal:

I can help your {business type} improve your online reputation. Your customers are seeing what others have to say about you before ever walking through your door - and the bad apples leaving these reviews are ruining your good name online. In fact, nearly 70% of your potential customers are consulting reviews and ratings before making a purchase decision. I'm sure if you had your way this isn't how you would choose to represent your company on the internet. I can work with you to suppress, directly answer, or in some cases entirely remove this negative press.

Costs? I can offer you services from a simple one-time cleanup to an ongoing monthly reputation management strategy. Whichever way you should decide to go, the costs involved are nothing compared to what this kind of negative customer-generated content is costing you every month. Just contact me on my cell at 00-000-0000. If I'm with another client just leave me a message and I'l get back to you as soon as possible.

Sincerely,

{Your Name}

The letter is short, sweet and straight to the point. You don't know how many buttons you just pushed in that owner's brain, but you have definitely got his/her attention. Make sure you sign this letter by hand, using blue ink (no handwriting fonts please, that's just unprofessional). Now, go back to that Google Maps page with their bad reviews and take a screen cap of those reviews. The key here is to fit as many as you can on one A4 piece of paper. Use Photoshop if you have to cut and paste many sections onto one page. Print that page out and find yourself a red marker pen. Write in capital letters on the page something along these lines: *"You have 10 '1-star' reviews on the very first page of Google – This is what your potential customers see when they search for your business!!!"*

Circle the worst parts of these reviews and make sure you're driving the point home. At this stage you are trying to break them down. You want them to get that sinking feeling in their stomach when they read these reviews. Remember, a lot of these offline business owners have no idea whatsoever that they are being insulted and bad mouthed on the internet, so your letter comes as a shock to them.

Now for the fun and different part. Take your beautifully signed letter and the print out of the bad reviews and bundle them up into a standard envelope. Next, you'll want to get your hands on a pair of (red) six sided dice. Why? Let me tell you. The dice play two parts in this campaign:

1. They will make your standard envelope lumpy. Lumpy mail works better. I will explain in a minute.

2. The dice will also play as a token of differentiation between your letter and the thousands of other marketing letter the business will receive during the week.

Now take those dice and place them in the fold of your letter, so that when the owner opens up the envelope, the first thing they see are the dice. Immediately, you have introduced intrigue into the equation, and when you first meet them, you will be known as the dice guy/girl. Ok, let me explain why lumpy mail works. Once an envelope becomes bulky, it is now treated as a parcel. This will cost you a little more, but it's definitely worth it. Why? Because now you get a big barcode on your parcel and is less likely to be thrown out as marketing mail, because it looks like a parcel to the owner of the company.

Make sure you hand address the envelopes and use a personal return address (not a business address) so that your parcel now looks like a personal gift and not marketing mail.

I'm going to take a leap of faith here and assume your jaws are dropping and you think this is absolutely the smartest thing you've ever heard, right? Good! Don't worry, it doesn't end here. I still have much more to say on the subject of Reputation Management.

Let's move onto fulfilling your duties as an ORM consultant. We know that we will be providing our client with two things:

1. 4x6 postcards
2. A landing page for their clients to use as a review portal

This is what the process will look like for your client:

- The business owner will hand a postcard to their clients as they leave their business (in this case, let's say it's my friend's restaurant)
- The owner will ask as a "personal favor" for the customer to review the business
- The owner will quickly walk them through the card and point out that it is an online review.
- When the customer gets home and follows the link to the portal, they will have two options: 1) Good review or 2) Bad review.
- Bad reviews will be sent directly to the owner (in real time) and good reviews will be directed to one of the many online profiles of the owner's business such as: Google Places, Yahoo Locale, Trip Advisor, etc…This way, only the good reviews will be captured online.

Let's quickly take a look at the psychological triggers at play here:

- Complainers want to be heard. They want to vent their frustration to someone of importance in the business, so why not give them a forum for their frustration. A simple form which will allow them to say everything they want to say directly to the owner of the business?
- They want someone to listen and acknowledge their pain (or bad experience)

- We are not denying them of this. We are just redirecting the negative feedback to a private email address (away from Google Places, etc...)
- Not only is the complaint heard, but the owner now benefits with a free audit of his business, and with the information received, can now make perfect changes to his/her business.
- If you don't already know, satisfied customers don't usually notify us of their satisfaction. They may thrown in a word or two about how good the food was, but other than that, they are naturally expecting to be satisfied when they walk into a place of business, so this personal favor is requesting them to kindly voice their satisfaction to the rest of the world.

To make your life easier, I will include a full package which will include everything you need from this chapter on my blog (www.ramiel-ashi.co.nr). I cannot give you a full tutorial on how you are supposed install this material, as it would take forever. Some research on Google will give you the answers you need. Or you can ask a friend to help you out.

How to use the material

Postcard: Fill in the business name and custom URL for each client on the card before printing. If your ORM business picks up, then I suggest you create a custom URL for each client. If you're not ready to move to that step, then create one URL such as www.ramisORMbusiness.com/bobscafe (bobs café being my client's establishment.) Obviously you will create one of these for each of your clients and they will be unlimited, so you don't have to pay for new URLs. You will want to print out these post cards professionally at your neighborhood print shop. If not, then search for an online company that will print in bulk and deliver.

Landing Page: This is pretty much all set up for you and ready to use. Obviously you will just have to switch all the links to your customer's links, so you will put your customer's Google Places link, Trip Advisor link etc...

How much are you going to charge for your amazing ORM service?

No less than $399/month/client and you can go as high as $999/month/client - You need to be a smart judge on the spot. That means you need to look at the owner and judge him/her by the success of their business. If you think they can pay the $999/month. Then do it. You are saving their face when it comes to their online reputation. You deserve to get paid for it.

Be sure to request 60 days upfront payment (that's 2 months) before you even begin. You need to secure some money for your hard work.

You can up sell them as well for the card printing ($50/month per 500 postcards + shipping) If the customer wants to do their own printing, no problem! You are not making money off of the printing, so let them do what they please. The fact that you are kind enough to let them choose, almost always works in your favor. They will always allow you to do the printing for them, why? Because they're busy.

Now we're at the final stages of our campaign. I have one more vital piece of material I would like to discuss with you, that will be the backbone of your entire business. That piece of material is a white paper filled with statistics which you will use to prime your client and educate them of the service you are about to perform.

You want to present your client with solid statistics pertaining to what you're presenting. The statistics have to be from a valid and trusted source and once you have those, you can let the statics do the convincing. Let me tell you now. In any of my business ventures, or even my full time job, I have used research as my primary tool. It is my weapon when people start to ask questions. It shuts them right up. All of these statistics are freely available on the internet, and yet people ignore them. They will do the hard selling for you, and you're being given them for free. USE THEM!

In this case, I have put together an ORM whitepaper for you to use (which again, I will put up on my blog for you to download). However, the statistics may be slightly out dated, so you'll have to do a bit of updating if you feel the need to be up-to-date. What you'll want to do is send this whitepaper to your client before setting up an in person meeting. This is where your educating begins. You want them to be completely knowledgeable about the figures relating to ORM and the internet before you present your postcard and landing page idea to them face to face. In some cases, they may even call you to cancel the face to face, simply because the report itself was so convincing.

I know there will always be that 1% of you who will think this all sounds a little bit like a scam, but the let me share some statistics with you:

- 55% of internet users look at other people's reviews
- 82% of internet users trust customer reviews over expert reviews (this is so huge, when you're selling your service)

- 50% of ALL internet users over the age of 18 have left a review online
- Customers are actually willing to pay more for companies who have excellent reviews
- 78% of internet users believe reviews are the most credible form of advertising

The report goes into a lot more details. With charts and figures to support each statement. Once you prospect studies this material, it should become painfully obvious that ORM services are the way to go. Where are they going to go? To you! You're the main man when it comes to securing someone's online reputation. 24 hours a day, 7 days a week and 365 days a year!

Remember, do NOT mention your postcard and landing page idea until you are sitting face to face with your client. If they know how to do it before the meeting, then they no longer need you. The white paper does not mention you method. Just some statistics. The white paper I'm including for you is rebrandable, so you can include your own company name, and be sure to include the logo or name of your client, somewhere on the front page to make them feel that this is a personalized report for them. You will use the same report for everyone, but they don't know that.

Some final words before you close this book. You need to be creative. You need to be imaginative. Take what you've learned and the tools I have provided you with and expand on them. Yes, there is work involved in everything I've mentioned. Yes, you will need to get up from behind your computer screen and meet your clients, but if you make the idea your own, you're bound to feel much better about it.

Creative ORM input: Imagine if you could eliminate the postcard and landing page completely and offer your client a mobile application (which you will design for them using www.freelancer.com and get paid extra for) where the customer can review the business while they're sitting at their table? Or you give them an iPad to do the review? The possibilities are endless, you just need to open up a bit.

I truly hope you enjoyed the ideas and experiments in this book and if I get a good enough response, I'll think about writing more books in the future. For now however, I hope this book becomes a reference book in your library and you learned a thing or two from me. Thank you!

ABOUT THE AUTHOR

Rami El-Ashi (born March 8th, 1984), is a Palestinian entrepreneur, analyst, digital media marketer and versatile businessman who has a passion for life and innovative business concepts. He enjoys working with other like-minded people to monetize their creative ideas and navigate through the numerous business and creative challenges along the path to strategic growth. He has focused much of his career on oil investment analysis, sourcing in China, expansion of e-Commerce & communities online, development of virtual business models, new age technology, and digital media.

After graduating from Saint Martin's University, he began his career as a Joint Venture Portfolio Statistical Analyst for the world's largest oil company; Saudi Aramco, where he was quickly promoted to Investment Analyst. After having worked there for 3 years, he was enthusiastically hired by Jarden Corporation as a Sourcing Manager in their Hong Kong office.

On July 1st 2012, Mr. El-Ashi launched his latest company Bicubik Hosting; a leading provider of Domain Registration/Transfer, Shared Web Hosting, Openvz VPS Hosting, Virtuozzo VPS Hosting, Semi-Dedicated Hosting & Dedicated Servers.

As July 2012 came to an end, Rami was elected Partner of There Is No Sky LLC; a firm consisting of bright minds which take you where you want to be, in business, life, and beyond. Their currency is access, which compliments your desire to be prominent. By leveraging who they know and what they can access, they have the ability to pull the strings you need and make the priceless connections for you.

Mr. El-Ashi is currently pursuing his Pg.D in Financial Engineering at Stanford University. This executive program led by Stanford University's Faculty of Management Science & Engineering focuses primarily on the following core modules: Investment Science, Investment and Finance in China, Two sided Market: A new Model for Business Innovation, Credit Risk Management & Options Theories and Practice.

Rami has lived, worked and traveled to over 30 countries, with residences spread through Hong Kong, Egypt, Cyprus & Palestine.

www.ingramcontent.com/pod-product-compliance
Lightning Source LLC
Chambersburg PA
CBHW022014170526
45157CB00003B/1240